WHAT TO COOK & WHEN TO COOK IT

WHAT TO COOK &

GEORGIE MULLEN

WHEN TO COOK IT

BLUEBIRD

8 Introduction

14 Cook's Notes

18
SPRING

74
SUMMER

20 Seasonal Calendar

42 Feature: Wild Garlic

76 Seasonal Calendar

86 Feature: Globe Artichoke

To my dad, to whom I owe everything.

146
AUTUMN

148 Seasonal Calendar

162 Feature: Squash

210
WINTER

212 Seasonal Calendar

232 Feature: Sprouts

---

272 A Menu For Each Season

274 About Georgie

275 Acknowledgements

276 Conversion Charts

278 Indexes

INTRODUCTION

What to Cook and When to Cook It is a modern blueprint for cooking throughout the year. These are recipes for people who love to eat and love to cook, too. The ingredients are simple and honest because I believe that great produce doesn't need much. The best ingredients speak for themselves if we allow them to.

We can have everything, all at once, at any time. In some ways that is a wonderful thing; a sign of physical and technological advancements. But modern convenience means entire generations are growing up without knowing when and how our food is grown. I'm fiercely passionate about seasonality; it is at the heart of everything I do, everything I write, everything I eat. Eating with the seasons allows us to reconnect with the cycles of nature and our food sources. It takes us back to basics, back to what it is all about: food at its most delicious.

There is such a rich diversity of fruits and vegetables available at different times of year. We should celebrate that it is still possible to reflect the rhythms of the natural world on our plates. I find the impermanence of seasonal ingredients appealing, too. The urgency to enjoy each fruit or vegetable at its best, before the season passes, acts as a reminder to savour each mouthful. It makes me feel grateful for what I am eating.

Apart from my wistfulness surrounding seasonality, there are other, practical reasons to eat seasonally. Consuming food at its freshest, when it has been allowed to ripen naturally, means it tastes as it should; full of flavour, vitality and nutrients. We are more likely to buy locally and support our farmers, reducing the carbon footprint associated with transporting produce long distances and reconnecting ourselves with the source of our food. And, eating this way reduces the need for energy-intensive methods of food production, such as artificial heating and lighting, supporting sustainable farming practices.

Think about the foods you most want to eat for the weather you are in – fragrant juicy tomatoes and burrata on a hot day, a comforting root vegetable stew in the winter – and most likely, you would have picked something seasonal. It's our intuitive connection to nature. You can also take the seasonal calendar (that introduces each chapter in the book) with you on your weekly shops, but failing that, just have a look at what is discounted – it's likely to be the fruits and vegetables in season.

I didn't grow up with food as a central point of my life. We never sat at the table as a family and neither of my parents were cooks. I started cooking only because I had to. At 14 years old, my mother was diagnosed with early-onset Alzheimer's disease and the world as I knew it fell apart. She could no longer cook for me, and so I had to cook for us both. Quickly I found that cooking dinner became the most joyous part of my day. It soothed and comforted me; it was something I could control. I had a handful of recipe books, which I would open at a random page and cook whatever I found there for dinner that week. I cooked anything and everything, experimenting with ingredients and techniques, hungry to learn as much as I could. Everything I know, I owe to my recipe books, and so to be writing my first one feels endlessly special to me.

As soon as I was old enough, I started working as a kitchen porter. My passion for food continued to grow, but it was there I realized that working as a chef in a restaurant kitchen probably wasn't for me; I liked experimenting with food, inventing new dishes. In 2018 I started the Georgie Eats website, Instagram and cookery classes, as a way to share my recipes. Georgie Eats has morphed and shifted over the years but without losing sight of where it all began – it's the food I love to eat.

My love for cooking and eating has never wavered, nor has my passion for great produce. In this book, I have focused on the fruits and vegetables you'll be able to find in abundance within their seasons, as well as some less common ones – globe artichokes, wild garlic, samphire – which I urge you to experiment with. Cook with creativity and enjoyment. Food is for enjoying. The recipes are mostly vegetarian, as that is how I eat, but all are adaptable to suit other dietary preferences, if you wish.

Some cooks love to follow recipes exactly as they are written and some cooks like to go off-piste, adding their own flair to a dish. I don't mind what you do with these recipes, but I always encourage using what you already have before buying more. With practice comes intuition. Trust yourself! Play some music, relax into the process. What a joy it is to cook!

I hope you can return to my cookbook year after year, thumbing through the pages each season, folding down your favourite recipes. I encourage writing in it too – making notes for yourself with swaps and edits. These are your recipes now.

Enjoy them.

COOK'S NOTES

I like to include as much detail as I can in my recipes to make them as clear as possible, but if I included everything I wanted to write, they would be far too long. So, here are some notes on the ingredients and cooking methods that I mention frequently in my recipes. I hope they will take the guesswork away.

AQUAFABA
Useful for thickening sauces and perfect for whipping, aquafaba is the liquid you find in a jar or tin of beans. Because of its neutral colour, I recommend using only the aquafaba found in a jar/tin of chickpeas, cannellini beans or butter beans for the recipes in this book.

BEANS
Jarred beans are far superior to their tinned alternative, in flavour and in texture. Where beans are the main feature of a dish, I recommend using the jarred varieties, if you can. For recipes where the bean is blended, for instance in hummus, tinned beans will be sufficient.

COCONUT
Throughout this book, you will find coconut milk (coconut pulp and water, blended together and strained), coconut cream (made in the same way as coconut milk, but thicker and more intense, with a higher fat content) and creamed coconut (a semi-solid block, made from the coconut pulp). I have chosen them for specific reasons for each recipe, but they are mostly interchangeable with tweaking:
— One 400ml tin of coconut milk can be substituted with both coconut cream and creamed coconut. To use coconut cream, thin out one 160ml tin with water to make it up to 400ml. To use creamed coconut, chop 100g into small pieces and dissolve in 350ml of boiling water.
— You can substitute one 160ml tin of coconut cream within a recipe with creamed coconut. Chop 75g into small pieces and dissolve in 100ml of boiling water.

—Creamed coconut can be substituted for both coconut milk and coconut cream. For each 100g of creamed coconut, use 400ml of coconut milk and reduce the liquid or stock used within the recipe by 350ml. To use 160ml of coconut cream, reduce the liquid or stock used within the recipe by 100ml.

EGGS

I have only specified the size of eggs when it is important to a recipe. When size is not specified, I recommend medium eggs. I always choose eggs of the highest welfare I can find. For baking, make sure the eggs are at room temperature before using.

MILK

At home, I use both dairy and non-dairy milk interchangeably, depending on nothing more than my mood. For these recipes, if I'm using dairy milk, I opt for semi-skimmed and for non-dairy milk, a semi-skimmed or whole oat milk. Unless stated, you can use any milk of your choice. Just make sure your non-dairy milk is unsweetened when preparing savoury recipes.

OIL

I use the phrase 'a glug of oil' frequently throughout these recipes. I estimate my glug to be approximately two tablespoons. A 'good glug of oil' is approximately an extra tablespoon in addition to that. For recipes which state to using a neutral oil, I recommend vegetable oil, sunflower oil, groundnut, rapeseed or a light and mild olive oil. After deep or shallow frying with larger quantities of oil, let it cool completely, before straining it into an airtight container and storing in the fridge – it can be used one more time for future frying.

PARMESAN

For ease, I have mentioned Parmesan in my recipes, but you could substitute it for any hard cheese you like.

POTATOES

Unless I have suggested a particular variety of potato within a recipe, for instance Jersey Royal, I will usually recommend

either a floury or waxy potato. All recipes can be substituted for an all-purpose potato variety, if needed.
—Varieties of floury potatoes, for mashing, baking and roasting include: King Edward, Désirée, Sante and Cosmos.
—Varieties of waxy potatoes, for salads and boiling, include: Jersey Royal, Charlotte, Maris Peer, Colleen, Novella, Lady Cristl, Lady Felicia and Pink Fir Apple.
—All-purpose varieties, for most cooking methods, include: Maris Piper, Marfona, Robinta, Romano, Valor and Orla.

SALT

For recipes where I have stated 'salt', I recommend using a flaky sea salt, for its clean flavour. For recipes that state 'fine salt', use either a fine sea salt, or crush the flaky sea salt in a pestle and mortar. For finishing a dish, I will always use a flaky sea salt.

STEAMING

To steam, place a steaming basket in a large saucepan and fill the pan with water so that it sits just below the steaming basket. Bring the water to a boil and add the vegetable, or other foodstuff, to the steaming basket. Clamp on the lid and steam for the instructed amount of time, checking the water level in the pan occasionally, to make sure it isn't running dry.

STOCK

Most regularly I use a vegetable stock pot, which I dilute in 500ml of boiling water. For recipes calling for a small volume of stock, use a smaller amount of the stock pot diluted in the appropriate amount of boiling water, saving the rest of the stock pot in the fridge for later use.

For recipes using large quantities of stock and for where it provides the main flavour, for instance in a risotto, I will use a fresh homemade or shop-bought stock.

SUGAR

I have only specified particular varieties of sugar when it is important to a recipe. Most commonly I have simply used 'brown sugar', for which you can use any type of brown sugar, or 'sugar', when any sugar you already have in your cupboard will be sufficient.

SPRING

As the air softens and the sun lingers a little longer each day, I find myself drawn to the kitchen. The heavy, comforting dishes of winter give way to something lighter, brighter, fresher and more vital. The promise of a new season shifts how I like to cook. And the ingredients: peas so sweet you can eat them raw, a lightly buttered Jersey Royal, the earthiness still clinging to their skins. The heady smell of wild garlic, gently purple tips of asparagus, the sharp sweetness of rhubarb. There's an irresistible simplicity to this time of year and I love to embrace it.

EARLY SPRING

Rhubarb (forced)

Beetroot

Celeriac

Jerusalem artichoke

Leek

Purple sprouting broccoli

Spinach

Spring onion

Swede

Watercress

Wild garlic

LATE SPRING

Rhubarb (outdoor grown)

Asparagus

Cauliflower

Chicory

New potato

Leek

Purple sprouting broccoli

Spinach

Spring onion

Radish

Watercress

Wild garlic

Pea shoot

Pea

Salad leaves (lamb's lettuce, lettuce and rocket)

Samphire

Spring green

A Very Quick Asparagus Tart

On slow weekends, I have been known to make a batch of puff pastry from scratch, wanting to enjoy and understand the process. But on an average day, a shop-bought roll of puff pastry is a marvellous thing; limitless in its possibilities and just as good.

This zingy, buttery tart can be eaten straight from the oven, or allowed to cool and boxed up for spring picnics. What a perfect quick lunch.

Preheat the oven to 180°C fan/390°F/gas 6.

Combine the cream cheese, lemon zest, garlic, parsley and a good pinch of salt and black pepper in a mixing bowl. Beat until combined and creamy, then taste and adjust the seasoning, if needed.

Unroll your puff pastry sheet on a baking tray. Use a long, sharp knife to create an indent approximately 3cm from the edge of the pastry on each side of the rectangle, to create the crust.

Spread the cream cheese mixture over the middle of the puff pastry, right up to the crust. Lay the asparagus side by side on top of the cream cheese, spacing them evenly from end to end. Use a pastry brush to glaze the whole tart – both the asparagus and the pastry – with a little olive oil. Bake for 25–30 minutes, or until the asparagus is tender and the crust is deeply golden.

Finish the tart with an extra grating of lemon zest and a pinch of flaky salt. I chop it into slices and eat them warm, or let them cool and wrap them up for a springtime picnic.

CUTS INTO 6

- 150g full-fat cream cheese
- zest of 1 lemon, plus extra for garnish
- 1 garlic clove, minced
- 10g parsley, stalks and all, very finely chopped
- 320g ready-rolled puff pastry sheet
- 350g asparagus, woody ends trimmed
- olive oil
- salt and freshly ground black pepper

New Potato & Garlic Soup

This is like eating a bowl of hot, buttery mash. Comfort food in its purest form. New potatoes have a more waxy texture than their larger, more floury counterparts, which is part of their charm. It can make them harder to blend, however, so try to take the time to push them through a sieve, as I have outlined in the recipe. It makes for a gorgeous soup; a salute to springtime.

Melt the butter in a large saucepan over a low–medium heat. Add the shallots and a pinch of salt and fry for 4–5 minutes, or until soft and translucent. Add most of garlic, keeping 2 or 3 of the sliced cloves aside for the topping, and fry for a further 2–3 minutes, or until it has softened and is turning very lightly golden. You don't want to get too much colour on it.

Stir through the potatoes and pinch of salt to coat them in the butter, then pour in the vegetable stock and milk. Bring the pan to a simmer, then lower the heat slightly and cook for 12–18 minutes, stirring occasionally, or until the potatoes can be easily broken apart with a fork. Remove from the heat and use the back of a spoon to push the soup through a sieve 2–3 times, until it is silky smooth. This will take a while, but it is more than worth it. You could also use a hand blender to blitz it until it is just about smooth, but you mustn't blend the soup for too long here, as it can become gluey. If you would prefer a thinner soup, you can either make up a little extra stock to stir through or just use water. Taste and adjust the seasoning, if needed.

Meanwhile, heat a small frying pan over a low–medium heat and add enough oil to coat the bottom. Once hot, add the remaining garlic and the rosemary and fry for a minute or so, until the garlic is very slightly golden, then remove the pan from the heat and let them cook and crisp up in the residual heat.

Ladle the soup into bowls. Drizzle over a few spoonfuls of the garlicky rosemary oil, along with the crisp garlic and rosemary itself, and grind over a little black pepper. You can eat it with bread if you like, but I don't think it needs it. I love it just as it is.

SERVES 4

- 25g unsalted butter
- 3 banana shallots, finely sliced
- 12 garlic cloves, finely sliced
- 1kg new potatoes, peeled and roughly chopped
- 550ml vegetable stock
- 500ml milk
- extra virgin olive oil
- 2 sprigs of rosemary, leaves picked
- salt and freshly ground black pepper

Griddled Asparagus & Caper Salsa Toast

Last year my friends planted their first-ever batch of asparagus: tiny little wisps the width of a needle appearing through the soil. The asparagus plants take about three years to establish themselves, coming back slightly thicker each year, until they are ready to harvest. Even then, it's a delicate crop, needing to be harvested by hand. Seeing the asparagus in the soil gave me a newfound appreciation for it: it's a vegetable that deserves to be celebrated! To honour it here we are griddling it – the smoky char marks bringing out its nuttiness – and smothering it with a piquant salsa. Opt for smaller, thinner spears if you can – they tend to be less fibrous.

Any leftover caper salsa will keep happily in the fridge for 5 days, or more.

SERVES 2

1 bunch asparagus, woody ends trimmed
olive oil
2 slices of nice crusty bread
soft cheese (burrata, stracciatella, or cream cheese)
salt and freshly ground black pepper
a little grated lemon zest, to serve

CAPER SALSA
15g parsley, stalks and all, finely chopped
25g roasted almonds, finely chopped
2 tbsp capers, finely chopped
1 tbsp red wine vinegar
zest of 1 lemon
extra virgin olive oil

Start by making the caper salsa. Combine the parsley, roasted almonds, capers, red wine vinegar, lemon zest and a good pinch of salt in a small bowl. Pour over just enough extra virgin olive oil to cover the mixture and stir well (you could also make this in a food processor, but it's nice when it has some texture, so don't blend it until completely smooth). Taste and adjust the seasoning, if needed.

Heat a griddle pan over a medium-high heat. Combine the asparagus with a glug of olive oil and a good pinch of salt and black pepper in a mixing bowl and use your hands to give them a mix. Griddle the asparagus for 3–4 minutes each side, or until bright green and starting to char, but retaining a little bite. You could also do this under the grill or on the BBQ, or in a regular pan – you just won't get the char marks.

Toast the bread in the griddle pan (you could also do this in the toaster, but while the griddle pan is out, you might as well use it). Spread it with a good dollop of soft cheese and top with the griddled asparagus and a few spoonfuls of caper salsa. Finish with a grating of lemon zest and a good crack of black pepper. You'll probably need a knife and fork.

Cheese Fondue, Jersey Royals, a Pickle of Pickles

I can't think of a better way to catch up with friends than over a bubbling dish of melted cheese. It's dipping and eating, pure communal food. The classic dippers are slices of French stick but I love the waxy texture of the Jersey Royals against the soft silky cheese. The pickle of pickle gives each mouthful a zingy lift too – essential in my opinion.

SERVES 4-6

400g Brie, rind removed, cubed
200g cream cheese
2 tsp cornflour
2 tbsp dry vermouth
1 garlic clove, peeled
1 sprig of rosemary
750g Jersey Royals
salt and freshly ground black pepper

PICKLE
120g cornichons, finely sliced
handful of parsley, leaves picked and finely chopped
2 tbsp white wine vinegar
2 tbsp extra virgin olive oil
2 tsp wholegrain mustard
2 tsp caster sugar

Preheat the oven to 140°C fan/320°F/gas 3.

Combine the Brie, cream cheese, cornflour, vermouth and a pinch of salt and black pepper in a food processor. Blitz to combine – it doesn't have to be completely smooth. Spoon into a small baking dish or a small ovenproof frying pan, and nestle the garlic and rosemary into the middle. Smooth over the top, then bake for 25–30 minutes, or until the surface is deeply golden and the cheese is bubbling. If it's not getting as golden as you'd like, you can pop it under the grill, to finish it off.

Meanwhile, bring a large pan of salted water to the boil. Add the Jersey Royals and bring the water back to a boil. Cook for 12–16 minutes, or until they are easily pierced with a fork. Drain and let them steam dry.

While the potatoes are boiling, you can make the pickle of pickles. Combine the cornichons, parsley, white wine vinegar, extra virgin olive oil, wholegrain mustard, caster sugar and a good pinch of salt in a bowl. Give everything a stir, then taste and adjust the seasoning, if needed.

Slice each Jersey Royal in half and arrange them in a dish to serve on the table. Spoon the pickle into a little bowl and pop that on the table too. When everyone is ready to eat, remove the fondue from the oven and place it in the middle of the table. Use forks to dip the Jersey Royals in the fondue and spoon a little of the pickle on top. If you're eating slowly, you might need to return the pan to the oven, to melt the cheese again. But normally, it's been gobbled up before that.

Purple Sprouting Broccoli Tempura & Lime Pickle Mayo

I love this dish. The tempura is perfectly spiced and the lime pickle mayo is, if I say so myself, inspired. Watch as everyone's eyes grow wide as they chew – it's that kind of recipe.

The key to perfect light, crisp tempura batter is, firstly, to make sure your sparkling water is ice cold; secondly, to not overmix your batter; and thirdly, and most importantly, to get your oil to the right temperature. If you have a thermometer, the oil should be approximately 175–190°C (350–375°F) before you start frying. If you don't (I never use one), the best way to test is to drop a small amount of batter into the oil – it should immediately bubble up and float. If the oil gets too hot, the batter will burn before the purple sprouting broccoli has cooked through. Test the temperature out with the first few and you'll get there. It's all just trial and error.

~~~~~~~~~~~~~~~~~~~~

Start by making the lime pickle mayo. Combine the mayonnaise, lime pickle, a pinch of salt and a few grinds of black pepper in a small food processor. Blitz until smooth and combined, then taste and adjust the seasoning, if needed. If you don't have a small food processor, or a smaller bowl in a regular food processor, you can combine the ingredients in a jug and use a hand blender. Taste and adjust the seasoning, if needed, blending through extra lime pickle, if you'd prefer a stronger flavour.

Next, get the oil ready. Heat 5cm of neutral oil in a medium pan over a medium heat. Let it get hot while making the batter.

Combine the flour, curry powder and a good pinch of salt in a mixing bowl. Whisk as you add the sparkling water, until you have a smooth batter. It's a thin batter; that's how you want it!

Dip each broccoli spear into the batter and get it well coated, then gently drop it straight into the hot oil. If the oil is spitting, add a good pinch of salt, which should stop it. You only want to have about 5–6 broccoli spears in the oil at any one time. Fry them until golden and crunchy on both sides, testing out the first few to make sure the batter isn't frying too quickly, leaving the broccoli uncooked inside. They should take about 3 minutes each. (If it is much quicker than this, turn the heat down.) Remove each one from the oil when it is ready, transferring to kitchen towel to soak up any excess grease.

Pile the broccoli tempura up on a plate and sprinkle them with flaky salt. Serve with the lime pickle mayo on the side, for dipping, and double dipping.

SERVES 4, TO START OR AS A NIBBLE

neutral oil
200g plain flour
2 tbsp mild curry powder
400ml cold sparkling water
500g purple sprouting broccoli, any really large stems sliced in two
salt and freshly ground black pepper

LIME PICKLE MAYO
125g mayonnaise
2 tbsp lime pickle

My Farinata with Asparagus & Peas

I've based this on the Italian farinata, a pancake made from chickpea flour (you may know it better as gram flour). It's a surprisingly easy dish to make, you just have to wait a while for the batter to rest, which I think is more than worth it. It is crisp on the edges, with a soft custard-like centre. A rather lovely lunch for spring.

SERVES 2, FOR LUNCH

150g gram flour (chickpea flour)
425ml lukewarm water
extra virgin olive oil
small handful of basil, leaves picked and finely chopped
small handful of chives, finely chopped
100g asparagus, woody ends trimmed and chopped into 7–8cm pieces
100g peas (fresh or frozen, whatever you have)
2 spring onions, finely chopped
25g salted butter
150g ball of burrata
salt and freshly ground black pepper
a little grated lemon zest and juice, to serve

Start by making the farinata batter. Sift the gram flour into a mixing bowl. Slowly pour in 425ml of lukewarm water, whisking as you go, until you have a smooth, pale yellow batter. Cover the bowl with a tea towel and let it rest for 3 hours, or for up to 8.

Preheat the oven to 250°C fan/520°F/gas 9 (or the highest heat your oven will go).

Once the batter has rested, heat a good glug of extra virgin olive oil in your best, large ovenproof frying pan over a high heat; one that doesn't stick. I use a 30cm cast iron or stainless steel one. Once hot, whisk the basil, chives and two good pinches of salt through the farinata batter, then pour it into the hot pan. The batter needs more salt than you think – it's a good idea to taste the raw batter here and adjust accordingly. Let it bubble and sizzle for 1 minute, then transfer the pan to the hot oven and bake for 15–20 minutes, or until the surface is golden.

Meanwhile, heat a good glug of olive oil in another large pan over a medium heat. Once hot, fry the asparagus and a pinch of salt for 2–3 minutes, to slightly soften. Add the peas and spring onions and fry for a further 2–3 minutes, until both the asparagus and peas are bright green and tender. Add the butter and stir it through, until it has melted.

Run a knife round the edge and the underneath of the farinata, then turn it out onto a serving plate. Tear open the burrata and arrange it on top, along with the buttered veg. Grate over a little lemon zest and a squeeze of juice, if you like. Finish with a crack of black pepper, then both dig in, sharing the same plate; fighting over the last bite.

Charred Peas, Mint, Chilli, Ricotta

I'm seeing crisp, sweet peas in their pods in the shops less and less, so, when you can find them, buy as many as you can carry. If you know someone who grows them, even better! Hold on to them tight – picking a pod straight off the plant and popping it into your mouth is one of life's greatest pleasures.

If peas in their pods aren't an option, podded peas will work too. They will only need about 2–3 minutes of frying in total. If you are using frozen peas, they will need an extra minute on top.

This works as a stand-alone dish, mopping up the plate with a slice of good crusty bread. You could serve it on the bread too, if that is what you fancy. Served without the ricotta, it also works beautifully as a side dish alongside my Tartiflette for Spring (see page 61).

SERVES 2 FOR LUNCH, OR 4 AS A SIDE

olive oil
400g peas in their pods
large handful of mint, leaves picked
1 red chilli, deseeded and finely chopped
zest of 1 lemon and juice of ½
150g ricotta
extra virgin olive oil
salt and freshly ground black pepper
extra lemon zest, to serve

Heat a large frying pan over a high heat and add a good glug of olive oil. Once hot, add the peas, in their pods, and a pinch of salt and let them sizzle and blister for 2–3 minutes on each side, until bright green and blackened in places.

Combine the charred peas, mint, chilli, lemon zest and juice and a pinch of salt in a mixing bowl. Give everything a good stir, then taste and adjust the seasoning, if needed.

Spread the ricotta on a serving plate. Spoon the marinated peas on top, then drizzle with a glug of your best extra virgin olive oil and finish with a crack of black pepper and an extra grating of lemon zest, if you like.

Springestrone

SERVES 4

olive oil
5 spring onions, finely sliced
3 garlic cloves, minced
½ tsp dried chilli flakes
400g tin cannellini beans, drained and rinsed
150g conchigliette (or any other smallish pasta shape)
1.5 litres good quality vegetable stock
200g fresh or frozen peas
250g asparagus, woody ends trimmed, stems finely sliced and tips kept whole
100g spring greens, shredded
handful of mint leaves, finely chopped
handful of parsley, hard stems removed, finely chopped
salt and freshly ground black pepper

TO SERVE
a little grated lemon zest
grated Parmesan

The name is a bit kitsch, I know. It's a minestrone for spring – spring vegetables, a little spice, pasta and handfuls of herbs. Vibrant and soothing.

I like my veggies – particularly the asparagus – to keep a slight crunch, to contrast between the soft and silky pasta. If you would prefer for yours to be softer, add the veggies in to cook a few minutes earlier.

Heat a good glug of olive oil in a large pot over a medium heat. Once hot, add the spring onions, garlic, chilli flakes and a good pinch of salt and fry for 2–3 minutes, until the whites of the spring onions are turning translucent.

Add the cannellini beans, conchigliette, vegetable stock and a good pinch of salt, stir well and bring everything to a boil. Lower the heat to a gentle simmer, cover the pan with a lid and cook, stirring regularly to stop the pasta sticking to the bottom of the pan, for 8–10 minutes, until the pasta is just about al dente.

Add the peas, asparagus and spring greens and bring the pan back to a simmer. Cook for a further 3–4 minutes, until the vegetables are bright green and tender, adding extra stock (or just boiling water) if the pan becomes too dry at any point. Taste and adjust the seasoning, if needed, then remove from the heat. Stir most of the fresh mint and parsley through the springestrone, saving some for serving.

Ladle the soup between bowls. Finish with the remaining herbs and a crack of black pepper. Grate over a little lemon zest and a generous amount of Parmesan and watch it melt into the broth.

Soupy Pasta Goodness

I have been making this recipe for many years. It's one of the few recipes in this book that I have taken from my website because it is a favourite with my readers. It's not quite a soup; it's not quite a pasta dish. It has some big flavours – umami sundried tomatoes, garlic, chilli, lemon. And, a seasonal luminary: the spring green, which is a favourite of mine.

This recipe is a nice one to transcend seasons. You can easily swap the spring greens for another green of your choice. Spinach in summer, cavolo nero in autumn, kale in winter.

SERVES 4

280g jar sundried tomatoes
1 onion, finely chopped
5 garlic cloves, minced
1 red chilli, deseeded and finely chopped
1 tsp dried oregano
225g dried pasta (any smallish shape)
1 litre vegetable stock
150g spring greens, very finely sliced
500ml milk
salt and freshly ground black pepper

TO SERVE

small handful of basil, leaves picked
grated Parmesan
a little grated lemon zest and juice

Pour a good glug of oil from the sundried tomato jar into a large saucepan set over a medium heat. Once hot, add the onion and a pinch of salt and fry for 6–8 minutes, stirring regularly, until soft and translucent. Add the garlic and chilli and cook for a further minute or so, just to soften.

Meanwhile, drain the sundried tomatoes from the rest of their oil and finely chop, into a rough paste.

Add the chopped sundried tomatoes and oregano to the pan. Continue to cook for a further 5–6 minutes, stirring regularly, until the sundried tomatoes are beginning to break down.

Stir through the pasta and pour in the stock. Bring everything to a boil, then reduce the heat to a simmer and cook for 8 minutes, stirring regularly to stop the pasta sticking to the bottom of the pan, until the pasta is al dente. Add the spring greens and bring the pan back to a simmer. Cook for a further 2–3 minutes, to wilt the greens. The pan will look reasonably dry – this is what you want.

Finally, pour the milk into the pan and stir it through. Remove from the heat, then taste and adjust the seasoning, if needed.

Ladle generously into bowls. Finish with the basil, a good grating of Parmesan, lemon zest, a squeeze of lemon juice and a few cracks of black pepper. Devour.

SPRING 35

Beans al Limone with Asparagus & Peas

The classic Italian dish pasta al limone inspired this recipe. It is in my opinion the most elegant of pasta dishes; a celebration of simple, good-quality ingredients. Here we have lemon singing loud and clear, with our tender spring vegetables backing her up. I like to eat it on a mild spring evening, maybe on the first night I sit outside for the year.

SERVES 2

olive oil
4 garlic cloves, minced
700g jar butter beans
300g asparagus, woody ends trimmed
100g fresh or frozen peas
1 lemon, pared into long strips and juiced
4 tbsp crème fraiche
35g Parmesan, finely grated
salt and freshly ground black pepper

TO SERVE
extra grated Parmesan
crusty bread

Heat a good glug of olive oil in a large pan set over a medium heat. Once hot, add the garlic and fry for a minute or so, just to soften. Add the beans, with their liquid, and a pinch of salt and stir well to combine. Bring the pan to a gentle simmer, then reduce the heat to low and cook for 5–6 minutes, stirring regularly, until the beans are ultra tender.

Meanwhile, heat a good glug of oil in another large pan over a medium heat. Once hot, add the asparagus and a pinch of salt and cook for 3–4 minutes, turning regularly, until they have gained some colour. Add the peas, lemon zest and a good crack of black pepper and continue to cook for a further minute or so, until the asparagus has blackened in places and the peas are bright green and tender. If your peas are frozen, they will need an extra minute or so.

Stir the crème fraiche, Parmesan and lemon juice through the beans. Taste and adjust the seasoning, if needed, then remove the pan from the heat.

To serve, arrange the asparagus, peas and lemon zest on top of the beans (you won't want to eat the lemon zest, so remove it before eating, but it looks too good not to serve). Finish with a good grating of Parmesan and a few cracks of black pepper. Serve with crusty bread on the table, to dip and scoop.

Lemongrass, Coconut, Noodles, Greens

Inspired by Malaysian laksa, this is soupy, noodly nirvana. Swap the tofu puffs for another choice of protein, if you like.
(See photos overleaf.)

SERVES 4

neutral oil
450ml vegetable stock
400ml tin coconut milk
½ tsp sugar
200g deep-fried tofu puffs, halved
150g purple sprouting broccoli, halved
150g asparagus, hard ends trimmed and halved
180g flat rice noodles
salt and freshly ground black pepper

CURRY PASTE

1 tsp cumin seeds
2 tsp coriander seeds
4 spring onions, trimmed and greens/whites separated
4 garlic cloves, peeled
large thumb-sized piece of ginger (don't bother peeling it)
2 sticks lemongrass (fresh is best, but dried if not), trimmed
3 green chillies, deseeded
50g coriander, stalks and all

TO SERVE

handful of coriander leaves
lime wedges

Heat a small dry frying pan over a low–medium heat. Once hot, add the cumin and coriander seeds and toast for a minute or two, stirring frequently, until they slightly darken and release their fragrance. Watch them carefully here as they can turn from browned to burnt in a matter of seconds. Remove from the heat and let them cool.

Combine the toasted cumin and coriander seeds, the whites of the spring onions, garlic, ginger, lemongrass, green chillies, coriander and a good pinch of salt in a food processor or blender. Blitz the mixture, scraping the sides of the bowl a few times if needed, until you have a smooth paste. If your food processor requires a little dash of water to help it along, that's fine. You just want to try and get the paste as smooth as possible.

Next, heat a good glug of neutral oil in a large pan over a medium heat. Once hot, add the curry paste and cook for 3–4 minutes, stirring constantly, until it fills the room with its perfume and has slightly darkened in colour. Add the vegetable stock, coconut milk, sugar and a good pinch of salt and black pepper, then bring everything to a gentle simmer. Lower the heat slightly and cook for 6–8 minutes, stirring regularly, until the sauce has reduced a little, but is still brothy. Add the tofu puffs and stir for a further 3–4 minutes, to warm them through. It's a thin sauce, but this is how you want it. The tofu puffs will suck it up nicely.

Meanwhile, use a steamer or steaming basket to steam the purple sprouting broccoli and asparagus for for 4–5 minutes, or until the greens are just tender. At the same time, you can cook your noodles according to the packet instructions.

Pile the noodles between bowls and ladle the laksa sauce and tofu puffs on top, letting the sauce pool around the sides. Finish with the steamed purple sprouting broccoli and asparagus, the finely sliced greens of the spring onions, fresh coriander and a few good grinds of black pepper. Serve with the coriander leaves and a few lime wedges each to squeeze over the top before tucking in.

Spring Pea Risotto

A proper springtime dinner. A celebration of peas! I've kept the pea flavour pairing very traditional here – mint, lemon. They brighten the peas, highlighting their natural sweetness. I like making this for friends – a perfectly made risotto is an impressive and wonderful thing.

Start by making the pea purée. Melt 10g of the butter in a large heavy-bottomed pan over a medium heat. Once melted, add 250g of the peas and a good pinch of salt and fry gently for 2–3 minutes, until the peas are bright green and tender (if you are using frozen peas, you might need an extra minute or so). Transfer into a high-speed blender, along with a ladleful of the stock, and blend until smooth and velvety.

Next, heat the same pan over a low–medium heat and add a glug of olive oil and 25g of the butter. Once hot, add the shallots and a pinch of salt and fry for 4–5 minutes, stirring frequently and being careful not to let them gain any colour, until soft and translucent. Add the garlic and fry for a further minute or so, just to soften.

Stir through the rice to coat it in the oil. Cook for a further 2 minutes, or until the rice turns a little translucent. Pour in the white wine and allow it to simmer and bubble for a minute or so, until almost evaporated.

Add a ladleful of the hot stock to the pan and stir continuously. Once all the liquid has been absorbed into the rice, add another ladleful of stock. Repeat this step, stirring continuously between ladlefuls of stock, until the rice is creamy but still slightly al dente (if you run out of stock, you can either make up a little more or just use boiling water. We are about to add more liquid, so don't worry if your risotto seems a little on the thick side). This should take you about 30 minutes, so grab yourself a drink. Lean into the process – it can be beautifully cathartic.

Remove the pan from the heat. Stir the pea purée, Parmesan, remaining whole peas and remaining butter through the risotto, until the peas are tender and the Parmesan has melted in the residual heat. Taste and adjust the seasoning, if needed.

Ladle the risotto between bowls. Finish with a swirl of your best extra virgin olive oil, a handful of pea shoots, a grating of Parmesan, a few fresh mint leaves and a little lemon zest. Squeeze over a splash of lemon juice, just before serving.

SERVES 4

- 80g unsalted butter
- 350g fresh or frozen peas
- 1.5 litres hot, good quality vegetable stock
- olive oil
- 3 banana shallots, finely chopped
- 3 garlic cloves, minced
- 300g risotto rice (Carnaroli is my favourite)
- 175ml dry white wine
- 25g Parmesan, finely grated
- salt and freshly ground black pepper

TO SERVE

- extra virgin olive oil
- handful of pea shoots
- extra grated Parmesan
- handful of mint leaves
- a little grated lemon zest and juice

WILD GARLIC

FORAGING 101

Wild garlic is one of my most favourite ingredients. Maybe because it feels so elusive. You have to ask around for secret spots and when you go looking for it, you never seem to be able to find it. So here are my top tips for wild garlic beginners.

1. Wild garlic grows mostly in damp, wooded areas and shaded hedgerows. Ask around friends or post on forums in your area to see if anyone has any good spots.

2. In the UK, it's best to pick it between March and early May, as the plants tend to become slightly bitter after that.

3. Carry a picture on your phone with you to help you remember what it looks like. Several plants look similar to wild garlic, but the main easily identifiable difference is that wild garlic smells strongly of garlic. Between April and June, it grows small, white six-petalled flowers, which are also edible. Remember, if you aren't one hundred per cent sure and you can't smell garlic, please don't pick it.

4. Try to pick the leaves away from the beaten track and avoid any situated right by a road.

5. Wash the wild garlic leaves thoroughly 2–3 times, to ensure they are clean. From here you can use them raw, or blanch them in boiling water for 10 seconds or so, which will help preserve their colour and slightly soften their flavour. The flowers just need a good wash and can be used as a pretty garnish.

Wild Garlic Pesto

When I find a good crop of wild garlic, I'll make a few batches of this, keeping some in the fridge and freezing the rest. Raw wild garlic leaves won't keep for very long; making them into a pesto is the easiest, most versatile way to preserve their strong, ephemeral flavour for longer.

MAKES APPROX. 1 X 350ML JAR

50g pine nuts
100g wild garlic leaves, hard stems removed, washed thoroughly
50g Parmesan, grated
juice of ½ lemon
100–150ml extra virgin olive oil
salt and freshly ground black pepper

Heat a small dry frying pan over a low heat. Once hot, add the pine nuts and toast for 2–3 minutes, stirring frequently, until lightly golden.

Combine the toasted pine nuts, wild garlic leaves, Parmesan, lemon juice and a pinch of salt and black pepper in a food processor. Blend, adding the olive oil in a slow drizzle through the tube in the top, until almost smooth (I like it to retain a little bit of texture). Taste and adjust the seasoning, if needed.

Transfer into an airtight container and refrigerate, or freeze, until ready to use.

WILD GARLIC PESTO – 3 IDEAS:

SPRINGTIME PIZZA: Spread liberally over pizza dough, top with mozzarella and your favourite green spring veg (peas and asparagus work well). Cook in a pizza oven, or a very hot kitchen oven, until the crust is crisp and the cheese is bubbling.

SANDWICHES: Spread over good ciabatta and top with jarred roasted red peppers and burrata or mozzarella. Eat toasted or untoasted.

EASY TARTS: Swap out the cream cheese base of my Very Quick Asparagus Tart on page 22 for a few good dollops of the pesto. You can swap the asparagus for any other spring veg too. Peas and purple sprouting broccoli are a good combination.

Silk Handkerchief Pasta with Wild Garlic Pesto

Another idea for your wild garlic pesto (see page 43). If you don't want to make your own pasta, simply use 450g of fresh lasagne sheets sliced into rough squares, and cook them as per the recipe. (See photos on previous pages.)

~~~~~~~~~~~~~~~~~~~~

Pile up both flours on a clean work surface and make a deep well in the centre. Sprinkle the flour with a pinch of salt, then gently crack the eggs into the well. Use a fork to gradually incorporate the flour from the sides of the well into the eggs, then as the mixture starts to thicken, use your hands to knead in the rest of the flour. Continue to knead the dough for 8–10 minutes, lightly dusting your work surface with flour if needed, until you have a smooth springy ball of dough. If your dough is struggling to come together, you can add a dash of water, 1 teaspoon at a time. Cover the dough with a tea towel and leave it to rest at room temperature for 30 minutes.

Divide the pasta dough into four and flatten each part with a rolling pin. Run each flattened section of dough through a pasta machine, starting at the thickest setting and gradually working your way down until the pasta sheets are approximately 1mm thick, dusting them with flour occasionally, to stop anything sticking. Spread the long sheets of dough on a lightly floured surface and slice into 15cm square-ish sections.

Next, warm the wild garlic pesto in a large frying pan over a low–medium heat.

Bring a large pan of salted water to the boil. Quickly drop the silk handkerchiefs in one by one and cook for 1–2 minutes, until al dente. Lift the pasta from its pan and into the pesto with a slotted spoon, bringing some of the pasta water along with it. Stir well to combine, adding a splash more pasta water to loosen everything up, if needed.

Let the silk handkerchiefs flop and fold between plates. They need nothing more than a lick of your best extra virgin olive oil and a crack of black pepper to finish, but if you have any wild garlic flowers left, they never go amiss.

SERVES 4

140g fine semolina flour
260g 00 flour, plus extra for dusting
4 medium eggs
1 batch of Wild Garlic Pesto (page 43)
extra virgin olive oil
salt and freshly ground black pepper
wild garlic flowers, if you have them, to serve

Risi e Bisi

Risi e bisi is a Venetian dish that translates simply to rice and peas. It's a simple, fresh, comforting cross between a soup and a risotto. There is a debate as to whether it should be eaten with a fork or a spoon. I vote spoon.

I like to make it with fresh peas in their pods, as it is traditionally made. You can make it with frozen peas too, if you like. Swap the peas in their pods for 400g of frozen peas, and use 1 litre of vegetable stock instead of the water.

~~~~~~~~~~~~~~~~~

Pod the peas, keeping the pods and the peas separate.

Combine the pea pods and half the mint stalks (you won't be using the other half of the mint stalks here, so you can save them for mint tea or compost them) with 1.25 litres of water and a good pinch of salt in a large saucepan and place over a medium heat. Bring to a boil, then reduce the heat to a simmer and cook for 15 minutes. This is the stock. Drain and discard the pea pods, keeping the liquid for use later.

Wash out your saucepan, return it to a medium heat and add a good glug of olive oil. Once hot, fry the spring onions and a pinch of salt for 4–5 minutes, until the whites of the spring onions are turning translucent. Stir through the rice to coat it in the oil. Cook for a further 2 minutes, or until the rice turns a little translucent.

Add a third of the pea stock and stir continuously for a minute or so. Add another third of the stock and again, stir continuously for a minute or so, as if you're making a very quick risotto. Add the last third of the stock, stir well and bring the pan to a gentle simmer. Cook for 8–10 minutes, stirring frequently, until the rice is al dente.

Stir through the podded peas and the mint leaves, then bring the pan back to a simmer. Cook for a further 6–8 minutes, or until the peas are bright green and tender and the rice has cooked through. It should have a thick brothy texture. If your pan becomes too dry at any point, you can add a little more liquid – just use boiling water from the kettle. Taste and adjust the seasoning, if needed.

Ladle the risi e bisi into bowls and drizzle with your best extra virgin olive oil. Grate over a little Parmesan and grind over black pepper. That is all it needs. It's simple, comforting food.

SERVES 4

600g fresh peas, in their pods
2 handfuls of mint, stalks kept whole and leaves picked
olive oil
5 spring onions, finely sliced
200g risotto rice (I like Carnaroli)

TO SERVE
extra virgin olive oil
grated Parmesan

Wild Garlic Gnudi

Gnudi look like gnocchi but are made with ricotta instead of potato. They take some time to make as they need to be chilled overnight, but the result is magical. Light, fluffy little clouds. The name refers to them being pasta-less, ravioli in the nude, without their coats. I first ate them in Florence last year, in their most traditional form of spinach and ricotta. I'm making them here with wild garlic, a balmy nod to spring.

This easiest ever one-pot tomato sauce recipe is based on one from Bee Wilson's *The Secret of Cooking*. It's a fantastic kitchen secret. Use it as a pasta sauce, a pizza base or for shakshuka.

~~~~~~~~~~~~~~~~~~~~

Decant the ricotta into a fine sieve and set it over a large bowl, or in the sink. Leave it to drain for an hour or two, until its liquid has drained away. You want it to be as thick and as dry as possible.

Next, heat a good glug of olive oil in a large frying pan set over a medium heat. Once hot, add the wild garlic and fry for 2–3 minutes, stirring constantly, until wilted. Remove from the pan and let it cool enough to touch. Finely chop, then use your hands to squeeze out as much water from it as you can. Don't skip the squeezing, it's important for the gnudi's structure.

Combine the drained ricotta, wild garlic, Parmesan, nutmeg and a good pinch of salt and black pepper in a mixing bowl. Give everything a good stir, then taste and adjust the seasoning, if needed. It's thick! This is what you want.

Line a baking tray with baking paper and spread the semolina in a shallow bowl. Take a tablespoon of the ricotta mixture and roll it between slightly damp palms, into a ball. Carefully roll it in the semolina, to coat the whole of the outside, then set it on the lined sheet. Repeat with the remaining mixture; you should end up with about 16 balls. Refrigerate your gnudi, uncovered, overnight.

To make the tomato sauce, combine the tinned tomatoes, butter, onion, sugar and a good pinch of salt in a medium saucepan set over a medium heat. Bring to a gentle simmer, then reduce the heat to low and cook for 35 minutes, stirring occasionally, until the sauce has reduced.

Recipe continues overleaf

SERVES 2

250g ricotta
olive oil
100g wild garlic, hard stems removed, washed thoroughly
50g Parmesan, finely grated, plus extra to serve
¼ tsp freshly grated nutmeg
50g fine semolina
salt and freshly ground black pepper

TOMATO SAUCE
400g tin whole plum tomatoes
50g unsalted butter
½ onion, peeled and chopped into wedges
½ tsp sugar

Remove the saucepan from the heat, then use a hand blender to blend it into a smooth and silky sauce (you can also do this in a stand blender, just let it cool down slightly first). Taste and adjust the seasoning, if needed.

When you are ready to serve, warm through the tomato sauce and bring a large pan of water to the boil. Cook the gnudi in two batches, dropping them into the boiling water, reducing the heat slightly and cooking until they float to the top. It should take about 3 minutes. Remove them from the pan with a slotted spoon and drain away any excess water.

Ladle the tomato sauce into a shallow bowl and tumble the gnudi over the top. Grate over a little Parmesan and finish with a crack of black pepper.

Purple Sprouting Broccoli & Tahini Beans

When I am beginning to despair about the lack of greens in season at the end of winter, purple sprouting broccoli arrives. A hardy crop, PSB can survive the lower temperatures in early spring. Riverford describes it as: 'vigorous, wild and woolly-looking, it's a delicacy equal to asparagus'. It's perfect roasted, as we are doing here – stems growing richer in flavour, florets and leaves getting crunchy. It makes a perfect contrast to the luscious, velvety butter beans.

~~~~~~~~~~~~~~~~~~~~

Preheat the oven to 160°C fan/350°F/gas 4.

Combine the broccoli, a glug of olive oil and a good pinch of salt and black pepper on a baking tray. Use your hands to give everything a mix, then roast for 18–22 minutes, or until tender all the way through and crisp at the edges.

Heat a good glug of olive oil in a large saucepan set over a low-medium heat. Once hot, add the garlic and fry for a minute or so, to soften, but not colour. Pour in the vegetable stock and the beans, with their liquid. Stir well to combine, then bring the pan to a gentle simmer and cook for 4–5 minutes, stirring occasionally, until the beans are soft and their liquid has reduced. The bean liquid (aquafaba) can be quite salty, so wait until the end to adjust the seasoning.

Meanwhile, combine the shallot, red chilli, cornflour and a pinch of salt in a mixing bowl and stir well to coat. Heat roughly a centimetre of olive oil in a small frying pan set over a medium heat. Once hot, fry the shallot and chilli for 2–3 minutes, until golden and crispy. Use a slotted spoon to remove them from the oil and onto a few sheets of kitchen towel, to soak up any excess grease.

Finally, stir the tahini and lemon juice through the beans. Taste and adjust the seasoning, if needed, then remove from the heat.

I like to serve these beans in their pan, topped with the roasted purple sprouting broccoli, the crispy shallots and chilli, and a spoonful of their cooking oil. Sprinkle with a few pinches of sesame seeds. Eat with slices of fresh crusty bread.

SERVES 2, GENEROUSLY

250g purple sprouting broccoli
extra virgin olive oil
4 garlic cloves, thinly sliced
100ml vegetable stock
700g jar cannellini beans
1 banana shallot, finely sliced
1 red chilli, finely sliced
1 tbsp cornflour
4 tbsp tahini
juice of ½ lemon
salt and freshly ground black pepper

TO SERVE
sesame seeds
crusty bread

Sausage, Borlotti & Spring Green Casserole

A wholesome stew for chilly spring days; one to eat while cosied under a blanket.

I very rarely eat any meat alternatives. I was never bothered by meat and so I don't feel the need. But there is something about the heartiness of a sausage that I love. The veggie alternatives are really fantastic, but you could also use good-quality, higher-welfare pork sausages here – the method will remain the same.

Heat a large heavy-bottomed pot over a medium heat and add a good glug of olive oil. Once hot, fry the sausages for 5–6 minutes, turning them regularly, until they have browned all over (they don't need to be cooked all the way through at this point). Remove them from the pan and set aside.

In the same pan, set over a low-medium heat, add the spring onions and a pinch of salt and fry for 3–4 minutes, until softened and the whites of the spring onions are turning translucent. Add a splash of extra olive oil here if you need to. Add the garlic, fennel seeds, rosemary and bay leaves and fry for a further minute or so, just to soften the garlic.

Increase the heat to high and pour in the wine. Allow to simmer and bubble for 2–3 minutes, or until mostly evaporated, scraping up any of the tasty bits from the bottom of your pan as you do. Return the heat back to medium, add the plum tomatoes and sugar and use the back of your wooden spoon to roughly crush them into the pan, breaking them up into the consistency of chopped tomatoes. Swirl a little water around the cans and add that too.

Pour in the borlotti beans and vegetable stock and stir well. Whisk in the cornflour slurry, then bring the pan to a simmer. Cook for 10 minutes, then lower the heat slightly, add the sausages and a good pinch of salt and cook for 20–25 minutes, stirring regularly, until the sauce has reduced into a beautiful silky stew and the beans are very tender. If your pan becomes too dry at any point, you can add a little more liquid – either make up more vegetable stock, or just use boiling water.

Finally, pick out the rosemary sprigs and bay leaves, then stir the spring greens, parsley and a few good cracks of black pepper through the stew, for 2–3 minutes, until wilted. Taste and adjust the seasoning, if needed.

Serve the stew in bowls, giving 2 sausages to each person, and finish with a crack of black pepper. You can eat it on its own, but I think crusty toast is essential for mopping up the sauce.

SERVES 4

- olive oil
- 8 sausages (I use vegetarian ones)
- 10 spring onions, finely sliced
- 4 garlic cloves, minced
- 1 tsp fennel seeds
- 3 sprigs of rosemary
- 2 bay leaves
- 200ml dry red wine
- 400g tin plum tomatoes
- 2 tsp sugar
- 400g tin borlotti beans, drained and rinsed
- 400ml vegetable stock
- 1 tbsp cornflour, mixed with 1 tbsp water to make a slurry
- 150g spring greens, hard stems removed, shredded
- handful of parsley, leaves picked
- salt and freshly ground black pepper
- crusty buttered toast, to serve

Purple Sprouting Broccoli, Orecchiette & Chilli Pangrattato

Purple sprouting broccoli is my favourite of the broccoli family. I love its sweet and earthy flavour, slender stalks and delicate, purple-tipped florets. This simple pasta dish is a wonderful way to showcase it, although, in the summer months, you could easily switch it out for the classic calabrese broccoli. It's a family dish – a great one for children too, just omit the hot sauce from the chilli pangrattato.

The chilli pangrattato is based on a recipe from *Crave* by Ed Smith. An inspired idea!

Start by making the pangrattato. Whizz the stale bread into rough breadcrumbs in a small food processor. Combine with the hot sauce, a glug of olive oil and a good pinch of salt and black pepper in a bowl and stir well, to coat them in the sauce. Place a small dry frying pan over a medium heat and once hot, fry the breadcrumbs for a few minutes, stirring frequently, until they are crunchy and darkly golden. Watch them carefully here – they can turn from golden to burnt in a matter of seconds.

Steam the broccoli for 8–10 minutes, or until it is really tender and is easily split into two with a butter knife. Let it cool enough to touch, then finely chop.

Next, cook the orecchiette in well-salted water according to the packet instructions, until al dente.

Meanwhile, heat a good glug of olive oil in a large frying pan over a medium heat. Once hot, fry the garlic for a minute or so, until slightly softened. Add the chopped broccoli, vegetable stock and a good pinch of salt and pepper and stir well to combine. Bring the pan to a gentle simmer and cook for 3–4 minutes, squashing the broccoli with your spatula as you stir, until the broccoli has broken down into a chunky purée and the stock has reduced completely.

Lift the pasta from its pan and into the sauce with a slotted spoon, bringing some of the pasta water along with it. Stir through the butter and Parmesan, until melted, then add a dash or two of extra pasta water to loosen the sauce, if it needs it. Taste and adjust the seasoning, if needed.

Serve the pasta between bowls and top with the chilli pangrattato, a grating of lemon zest and a good crack of black pepper. It's fork food. My favourite.

SERVES 2, WITH AN EXTRA PORTION FOR LUNCH

1 slice of stale bread (about 45g)
2 tsp hot sauce
olive oil
350g purple sprouting broccoli, roughly chopped
225g orecchiette (or any other short pasta shape)
6 garlic cloves, finely sliced
100ml vegetable stock
25g unsalted butter
25g Parmesan, finely grated
salt and freshly ground black pepper
a little grated lemon zest, to serve

Parathas, Paneer, Pickled Rhubarb, Green Chutney

This recipe is for sharing with friends, to laugh and gossip over. Put everything on the table and let everyone help themselves. Sweet and sour pickled rhubarb, verdant spicy chutney and a crisp creamy bite of paneer: perfection. You can swap the paneer for extra-firm tofu, if you like. (See photo overleaf.)

MAKES 8, TO SERVE 4

neutral oil
8 frozen parathas
200g thick plain yoghurt
salt and freshly ground black pepper

QUICK PICKLED RHUBARB
100g rhubarb, very finely sliced
100ml rice vinegar
1½ tbsp caster sugar
1 tsp mustard seeds
75ml boiling water

SPICY GREEN CHUTNEY
60g mint, leaves picked
30g coriander, stalks and all
1 green chilli, deseeded
juice of 2 limes
½ thumb-sized piece of ginger, peeled
1 tsp sugar
1 tsp cumin seeds

PANEER
450g paneer, cubed
1 tsp garam masala
2 tsp ground cumin
½ tsp ground turmeric
2 tbsp cornflour

First, make the pickled rhubarb. Combine the finely sliced rhubarb, rice vinegar, caster sugar, mustard seeds and a pinch of salt in a bowl. Use your fingers to massage the mixture into the rhubarb for a minute or so, until the rhubarb slightly softens. Add 75ml of just-boiled water, then give everything a stir. Let it sit and macerate while you continue with the recipe. Drain just before serving.

Next, make the green chutney. Combine the mint, coriander, green chilli, lime juice, ginger, sugar, cumin seeds and a good pinch of salt and black pepper in a food processor. Blitz the mixture, scraping the sides of the bowl a few times if needed, until you have a mostly smooth paste. If your food processor requires a little dash of water to help it along, that's fine. It should be the consistency of mint sauce – thick, but still easily spread. Taste and adjust the seasoning, if needed.

Combine the cubed paneer with the garam masala, ground cumin, ground turmeric, cornflour and a good pinch of salt in a mixing bowl and use your hands to give everything a good mix, to coat the paneer in the spices. Add more salt than you would normally here – paneer needs generous seasoning. Heat your largest frying pan over a medium heat and add enough neutral oil to coat the bottom. Once hot, add the paneer cubes and fry for 6–8 minutes, turning them every few minutes, until crisp and golden on all sides. Use a slotted spoon to remove them from the oil and onto a few sheets of kitchen towel, to soak up any excess grease.

While the paneer is frying, heat two or three lightly oiled frying pans over a medium heat. Once hot, cook a frozen paratha in each one for 3–5 minutes, flipping them every minute or so and using your spatula to press them down into the pan, until they are golden brown and crisp. You don't have to cook them all straight away. I'll usually eat my first paratha, then cook more for anyone who would like another one.

Serve everything on the table, alongside a bowl of thick plain yoghurt, and let everyone help themselves – filling their parathas, just as you would fajitas.

A Tartiflette for Spring

Tartiflette was originally created in the 1980s, to promote Reblochon cheese. It's since become a classic in the Alps – a rich, indulgent dish of potatoes, crispy bacon, sautéed onions and lots and lots of Reblochon cheese. This is my spring take on it, made using Jersey Royals and spring onions. You can add bacon if you like, but I don't think it needs it.

Preheat the oven to 200°C fan/425°F/gas 7.

Bring a large pan of salted water to the boil. Add the Jersey Royals, then bring the pan back to a boil. Cook for 8–10 minutes, or until the potatoes are easily pierced through with a knife, but are still holding their shape. Drain and let them steam dry.

Next, heat a large ovenproof frying pan over a low–medium heat and add a good glug of olive oil. Once hot, fry the spring onions gently for 5–6 minutes, or until starting to caramelize. Add the garlic and fry for a further minute so, just to soften.

Increase the heat to high and pour in the wine. Allow to simmer and bubble for 3–4 minutes, until mostly evaporated. Remove the pan from the heat.

Add the Jersey Royals, two-thirds of the Reblochon and a good pinch of salt and black pepper to the pan and give it a rough stir, to distribute the cheese evenly throughout the potatoes. Layer the rest of the Reblochon over the top and dollop randomly with the crème fraiche. Grind over a few good cracks of black pepper, then bake for 30–35 minutes, or until the top is deeply golden and the cheese is bubbling.

Serve the tartiflette to the table in its pan, for everyone to help themselves. It's lovely with a fresh zingy green salad, or with my Charred Peas on page 32. Just omit the ricotta.

SERVES 4

1kg Jersey Royals (or any other new potatoes), skins left on, quartered
olive oil
12 spring onions, finely sliced
1 garlic clove, finely sliced
200ml dry white wine
250g Reblochon cheese, roughly sliced
100g crème fraiche
salt and freshly ground black pepper

Spring Onion Scones & Jalapeño Cream Cheese

I've based this recipe on my mum's cheese scone recipe, which I found ripped out of a magazine, the paper curling at the edges. The jalapeño cream cheese is my addition – my mum would eat them simply with a thick slathering of butter and an extra lump of cheese. Both are wonderful, so take your pick.

Preheat the oven to 180°C fan/390°F/gas 6 and put a baking tray in the oven to warm up.

Sift the flour, English mustard powder and baking powder into a mixing bowl. Add the butter and a pinch of salt and black pepper and use your fingers to work it into the flour mixture, until you have something which resembles rough breadcrumbs. Stir through most of the grated Cheddar and most of the spring onions (keep a small handful back of each for topping), then add the milk and knead it together very briefly with your hands (careful not to overwork it) until the mixture forms a dough. It is a crumbly dough, but if it's too crumbly to come together, you can add a little more milk, 1 teaspoon at a time.

Gently roll out the dough on a floured surface into a disc shape roughly 2.5cm thick, then cut it into quarters and eighths, like you would a pizza. Lay each triangular scone on a sheet of baking parchment and brush with a little milk. Combine the remaining grated Cheddar and spring onions in a small bowl and sprinkle them over the top of each one. Grind over black pepper, then slide the whole sheet of parchment quickly onto the hot baking tray and bake for 15–20 minutes, or until they have risen and are golden on top. Let them cool for 5 minutes.

While the scones are cooling, you can make the jalapeño cream cheese. Combine the cream cheese, pickled jalapeños, Parmesan, lemon juice and a good pinch of salt and black pepper in a small bowl. Give everything a stir, then taste and adjust the seasoning, if needed. Refrigerate until ready to serve.

Tear or slice open the still slightly warm scones and slather with the jalapeño cream cheese. They are a wonderful thing.

MAKES 8

225g self-raising flour, plus extra for dusting
½ tsp English mustard powder
1 tsp baking powder
55g unsalted butter, chilled and cubed
125g Cheddar, grated
3 spring onions, finely sliced
90ml milk, plus extra for brushing
salt and freshly ground black pepper

JALAPEÑO CREAM CHEESE
175g cream cheese
40g pickled jalapeños, drained and finely chopped
25g Parmesan, finely grated
1 tbsp lemon juice

Soda Bread & Wild Garlic Butter

When I lost my mum, I found myself searching for anything and everything that connected me to her. Pictures, handwritten notes, foods she liked to eat. I hadn't had a slice of soda bread since I was a child, but I found myself buying it again. The exact brand she used to buy. And the potato farls she loved, too.

Not much of my mum's Irish heritage trickled into my childhood, only the food. We would eat warm toasted soda bread together, spread thickly with salted butter. Me sat at the table, her standing at the counter. We made it together a few times too, the whole loaf gone by the end of the day. This recipe is for her.

~~~~~~~~~~~~~~~~~~

Preheat the oven to 200°C fan/425°F/gas 7.

Combine the milk and lemon juice in a large jug and stir well. Let it sit for 15 minutes, so it thickens and slightly curdles.

Next, sift both the plain and wholemeal flour and the bicarbonate of soda into a mixing bowl. Tip in any bits of rusk left in the sieve too. Add a really good pinch of salt (1½ teaspoons is about right) and stir well to combine.

Pour the curdled milk into the dry ingredients and using a fork, bring them together into a rough dough. You want to work the dough as little as possible here, so as soon as the mixture is combined, leave it alone. Lightly flour a baking tray and use floured hands to lift the dough gently from the bowl and onto the floured tray. Pat the dough into a round loaf, about 20cm in diameter. Again, try to touch it as little as you can here, leaving it alone as soon as it is done.

Score a deep cross into the loaf with a sharp knife. Bake for 20 minutes, then reduce the oven to 180°C fan/390°F/gas 6 and bake for a further 12–18 minutes, until the soda bread is golden on top and the bottom sounds hollow when tapped.

Transfer the loaf to a wire rack and cover it with a tea towel, to keep the crust soft. Let it cool for 30 minutes. It will be a very challenging 30 minutes, but you'll end up with a better loaf.

Meanwhile, combine the butter and wild garlic in a food processor. Blitz until it has turned a vibrant green, but still has a little texture. Taste and add a pinch of salt if needed.

Tear the slightly warm bread into quarters and slather with more wild garlic butter than you thought possible. You must tear it; slices are just not the same. It is best to eat the bread the same day, but the butter keeps for a while in the fridge, or for much longer in the freezer.

MAKES 1 LOAF AND MORE BUTTER THAN YOU NEED

- 350ml whole milk
- 2 tbsp lemon juice
- 300g plain flour, plus extra for dusting
- 265g plain wholemeal flour
- 1½ tsp bicarbonate of soda
- fine salt

WILD GARLIC BUTTER

- 225g salted butter, at room temperature
- 75g wild garlic leaves, roughly chopped

Ricotta Stove Cakes, Honey-Poached Rhubarb

Forced rhubarb (sometimes called winter rhubarb) is in season in the UK between January and March and is known for its slender stalks and vibrant colour. It's grown in the dark which encourages it to grow quickly, producing a more refined and less fibrous texture. After March you'll be able to find outdoor-grown rhubarb, which is around until the beginning of summer. It's slightly less vibrant and sweet than its forced sister, but you can balance it out with a little extra sugar, if you need to.

For its lively pink, I like using forced rhubarb here. Think of these as mini pancakes: light, fluffy little things that are sweet, velvety and tangy from the ricotta. They are a weekend breakfast, or a special dessert for friends.

Start by making the poached rhubarb. Combine the rhubarb, honey and orange juice in a large saucepan. Stir well to combine, then place over a low–medium heat and bring to a gentle simmer. Cook for 5–8 minutes, stirring very occasionally, until the rhubarb is tender all the way through, but is still keeping its shape. Remove the pan from the heat, then pop on its lid to keep it warm while you continue with the recipe.

Combine the ricotta, egg, icing sugar, orange zest and a tiny pinch of salt in a mixing bowl and whisk until smooth and combined. Sift in the flour and fold it gently through the mix, until just combined.

Heat a large frying pan over a medium heat and add enough neutral oil to thinly coat the bottom. Fry heaped tablespoons of the mixture in batches for 2–3 minutes on each side, moulding them into little round mounds approximately 1–1.5cm thick with your spoon as you drop them into the pan, until they are gorgeous and lightly golden. You might need to add a little extra neutral oil between batches. Also, just be careful when you flip them, as they are quite fragile. Transfer to a plate and keep warm in a very low oven while you fry the rest of the mixture.

Serve a few of the ricotta cakes on each plate and spoon over the honey-poached rhubarb and a little of their poaching liquid. Finish with an extra grating of orange zest, if you like.

SERVES 4

500g ricotta
1 medium egg
2½ tbsp icing sugar
zest of 1 orange
small pinch of salt
80g plain flour
neutral oil

HONEY-POACHED RHUBARB
500g rhubarb, chopped into 7–8cm diagonal slices
4 tbsp runny honey
juice of 2 oranges

Rhubarb & Pink Peppercorn Crumble

I like to listen to podcasts or an audiobook on my daily walk with my dog, Poppy. One particular day, I was listening to Ardal O'Hanlon on the *Off Menu* podcast chatting about his dream meal. He mentioned his family tradition of making a rhubarb crumble with pink peppercorns and I had to stop, rewind and listen to it all again. I've played around with this recipe for a while, perfectly balancing the fiery ginger-like heat of the pink peppercorns with the tartness of the rhubarb. The result is gorgeous: an elegant twist on a classic pud.

The pink peppercorns must be crushed really finely, to distribute them evenly throughout the fruit. As you break them down, you'll notice the vibrant pink skin breaks away, revealing the brown-ish peppercorns inside – the harder part to crush. It's not a chore, however: their perfume is a treat.

SERVES 4, GENEROUSLY

800g rhubarb, chopped into 5cm chunks
200g brown sugar
juice and zest of 1 blood orange
2 tbsp pink peppercorns, crushed finely in a pestle and mortar
25g unsalted butter

CRUMBLE TOPPING
150g plain flour
1 tsp baking powder
110g unsalted butter, chilled and cubed
45g caster sugar
45g Demerara sugar
pinch of salt
chilled cream, to serve

Preheat the oven to 160°C fan/350°F/gas 4.

To make the filling, combine the rhubarb, brown sugar, juice and zest of the blood orange, crushed pink peppercorns and butter in a saucepan set over a low heat. Cook, stirring occasionally, for 10–12 minutes, or until the rhubarb is tender but still holding its shape. Transfer the filling to a pie dish and let it cool while you make the topping. My dish is 22 x 28cm, but slightly smaller is fine too.

To make the topping, combine the flour and baking powder in a mixing bowl. Add the butter and use your fingers to work it into the flour mixture, until you have something which resembles rough breadcrumbs. I find it helpful to rinse your hands with very cold water and dry them before you do this – it stops the butter melting quite so quickly, creating a better texture. Stir through the caster sugar, Demerara sugar and salt, then spread evenly over the rhubarb filling, trying not to flatten it too much.

Bake for 35–40 minutes, or until the crumble is golden brown and bubbling around the edges. Serve with cold cream. It's essential.

SPRING 69

Rhubarb & Custard Blondies

This is everyone's childhood favourite combination in blondie form. Use forced rhubarb if you can. It's in season in the UK between January and March and will reward you with the most gorgeous vibrant pink compote. If you miss it, outdoor-grown rhubarb will do the trick too – you could add a squeeze of red or pink food colouring to help the colour along.

Start by making the rhubarb compote. Combine the rhubarb, caster sugar and 2 tablespoons of water in a small saucepan. Clamp on the lid and place over a low–medium heat. Cook for 6–8 minutes, stirring occasionally, until the chunks of rhubarb have broken down into a thick compote. Remove from the heat and set aside to cool.

Preheat the oven to 180°C fan/390°F/gas 6 and line a brownie tin with parchment paper. My brownie tin is 21 x 21cm, but slightly smaller is fine too.

Next, combine the melted butter, sugar, egg, vanilla bean paste and a pinch of salt in a mixing bowl. Sift in the flour and fold gently, until fully combined. Stir through the chopped white chocolate, stealing a few chunks to nibble on while you do so.

Spread the batter in the prepared brownie tin and bake for 15 minutes.

Dot the cooled rhubarb compote and custard randomly over the top of the par-baked blondie. Use a butter knife to gently marble the compote and custard together, spreading them right up to the sides. Return the tin to the oven and bake for a further 10–15 minutes, until the custard has formed a skin on top and the blondie is golden around the edges.

Allow the blondies to cool completely in their tin, before chopping into slices and keeping refrigerated. You can eat them at room temperature when they are slightly gooey, but I prefer them straight from the fridge when they have turned fudgy and chewy. Both options are delicious, but see what you prefer.

CUTS INTO 9

115g unsalted butter, melted
190g soft light brown sugar
1 medium egg
2 tsp vanilla bean paste
pinch of salt
145g plain flour
150g white chocolate, roughly chopped
120g custard (from a tin or the posh stuff from a tub)

RHUBARB COMPOTE
200g forced rhubarb, chopped into 2cm chunks
40g caster sugar

Rhubarb Sour

Using aquafaba in cocktails is a genius way to get them to foam without using raw egg whites. It has a neutral flavour, so as not to disrupt the delicate sweet-sour flavour of the rhubarb, but best of all, it is a way to use up something you are likely to throw away.

Any leftover rhubarb syrup will keep in the fridge for up to 5 days or more, and is really wonderful stirred through thick plain yoghurt.

SERVES 1, WITH LEFTOVER SYRUP

50ml good quality gin
25ml lemon juice
25ml aquafaba (the liquid in a tin of beans)
1 rhubarb stalk, to decorate

RHUBARB SYRUP
4 large stalks of rhubarb, chopped into 2cm pieces
185g caster sugar
1 strip of lemon peel

To make the rhubarb syrup, combine the chopped rhubarb, sugar, lemon peel and 150ml water in a saucepan. Bring everything to a boil, then reduce the heat to a gentle simmer and cook for 6-8 minutes, stirring regularly, until the rhubarb is breaking apart. Remove the pan from the heat and let it cool completely before straining through a fine sieve. Any purée left in the sieve can be eaten over yoghurt, or if you are me, straight from the sieve. Refrigerate until ready to use.

When you are ready to make your cocktail, combine the gin, 25ml of the rhubarb syrup, lemon juice and aquafaba in a cocktail shaker. Add a handful of ice, then clamp on the lid and shake until the cocktail shaker has frosted on the outside. Strain into a coupe glass, then use a speed peeler to peel a thin strip of rhubarb to twist and curl and gently place on top. Enjoy immediately, while it is ice cold.

SUMMER

As the heat of summer settles in, during long, sun-drenched days, I am spoiled by the rich availability of my favourite fruits and vegetables. Tomatoes ripened by the sun, their skins warm and taut, sweetcorn grilled simply in its silk, fruits that seem to taste of the season itself – peaches, plums and berries so sweet they hardly need anything more than a spoon. Summer food is quick, intuitive and made for sharing. It's about allowing produce to speak for itself. There's a joy about it all – the less you do, the more you taste.

EARLY SUMMER

Strawberry

Asparagus

Broad bean

Kohlrabi

Pea

Pea shoot

Radish

Salad leaves (lettuce and rocket)

Samphire

Spinach

Wild garlic

New potato

Carrot

Chilli

Courgette (and other summer squash)

Cucumber

Fennel

Globe artichoke

Green bean

Pak choi

LATE SUMMER

Apricot

Blackberry

Blueberry

Cherry

Strawberry

Nectarine

Peach

Raspberry

Pea

Broccoli

Pepper

Salad leaves (lettuce and rocket)

Samphire

Runner bean

Sweetcorn

Tomato

Carrot

Chilli

Courgette (and other summer squash)

Cucumber

Fennel

Globe artichoke

Green bean

Aubergine

Radish Butter

I've taken inspiration from the French here, who like to eat their radishes dipped into butter and sprinkled with salt. My radish butter combines it all into one and is designed to be slathered generously over crusty bread – it's one of the best things you can eat.

MAKES APPROX. ONE 300G BLOCK

200g radishes (breakfast radishes are my preference, but classic, bulbous radishes will do the job too)
125g salted butter, softened
flaky salt
crusty bread, to serve

Top and tail the radishes and coarsely grate them with a box grater, then use your hands to squeeze out any excess liquid over the sink.

Beat the butter until smooth in a mixing bowl. Add the radishes and a good pinch of flaky salt, then stir well to combine. Taste and adjust the seasoning, if needed.

Spoon the radish butter onto parchment paper and wrap tightly into a log, or spoon into a Tupperware container and smooth over the top. Chill until the butter has set, then serve with lots of crusty bread and a pinch more flaky salt, if you like.

Balsamic Strawberries & Stracciatella

Sitting at the table as a child eating a bowl of strawberries and cream, I watched in horror as one of my parents' friends reached for the black pepper. I felt it was an unfair addition to a perfect dish: complete with only two simple ingredients. Many years on I still agree with my younger self; strawberries and cream need no innovation. But that doesn't mean there isn't room to play around with the concept itself. Here, I'm roasting strawberries with balsamic and black pepper, until rich and jammy, and serving them with cool, creamy stracciatella. It's a really sexy dish to serve with drinks. A savoury strawberries and cream.

I find stracciatella a bit of a pain to get hold of. If you can't find any, buy a ball of mozzarella, shred it apart with two forks and combine with two tablespoons of double cream in a bowl. Let it rest in the fridge for an hour or so and voilà! You'll have yourself a batch of DIY stracciatella.

MAKES 1 PLATE

500g strawberries, hulled and halved
1 tbsp balsamic vinegar
175g stracciatella
handful of basil, leaves picked
flaky salt and freshly ground black pepper
crusty ciabatta, to serve

Preheat the oven to 160°C fan/350°F/gas 4.

Combine the strawberries, balsamic vinegar and a good pinch of salt and black pepper in a baking dish large enough for the strawberries not to overlap. Give everything a good mix, then roast for 35–40 minutes, stirring halfway through, until the strawberries are jammy and syrupy.

Spread the stracciatella on a serving plate. Stir most of the basil leaves through the roasted strawberries, then spoon over the stracciatella. Drizzle with any syrupy liquid you have left in the tray and finish with a few cracks of black pepper, a pinch of flaky salt and the remaining basil leaves. I'll serve this pre-dinner, popping it on the table with a crusty ciabatta for my friends to scoop and dip.

Blistered Broad Beans with Chilli, Lime & Salt

An ideal pre-dinner snack: broad beans griddled until blistered and charred and smothered in chilli, lime and salt. Pop them on the table for friends to fight over. Give them a napkin too, because these are messy, but in the best possible way.

Combine the broad beans with a good glug of olive oil and a good pinch of salt in a mixing bowl. Use your hands to give everything a toss, to evenly coat the broad beans in the oil.

Next, you have two options. You can either heat up your BBQ to get it ready for cooking, or warm a griddle pan over a medium–high heat. Once hot, BBQ/griddle your broad beans for 3–4 minutes each side, until they have turned a vibrant green and have blistered and blackened in places.

Arrange the broad beans on a serving plate and drizzle generously with extra virgin olive oil. Grate over the zest of both limes, as well as a good grating of the frozen chilli (I normally use about ¼ of the chilli, then pop it back in the freezer for next time. But you can adjust this depending on how spicy you'd like the broad beans to be). Squeeze over the juice of one of the limes and finish with a really good pinch of flaky salt.

Eat the broad beans a little bit like edamame – covering your fingers with the seasonings on the outside of the pods as you search for the beans inside. Then, licking your fingers as you eat the beans, to get both the seasonings and the beans in one mouthful. You'll find the beans inside the pods in a white coating – the coating on the smaller, more tender beans will be fine to eat, but it can be a little bitter on the larger beans. Just squeeze the bean from its white coating and continue on as normal. You can even eat the pods of the smaller more tender broad beans, if you like.

SERVES 4, AS A PRE-DINNER SNACK

750g whole broad beans
extra virgin olive oil
2 limes
1 chilli, frozen until rock hard
flaky salt

Radishes Braised with Miso

I often joke that particular vegetables, or fruits, could do with a new PR team. Radishes don't get much love in our kitchens, apart from appearing in the occasional salad. But there is so much more they are capable of. Braised, like this, they are surprising and exciting.

I'll serve this as a side dish, as part of a larger spread. They are fantastic on rice bowls, or sushi bowls too. The timings here are written for breakfast radishes (sometimes called French radishes); if you're using the classic pink bulbous radishes, increase the cooking time by a few minutes.

Melt the butter in a large frying pan set over a medium heat. Arrange the radishes cut side down in the hot pan and sprinkle with a good pinch of salt. Cook, undisturbed, for 4–5 minutes, or until the bottoms of the radishes are a gorgeous golden brown.

While the radishes are frying, combine the miso paste, brown sugar and 100ml of just-boiled water in a bowl and whisk until smooth.

Pour the sauce into the pan and let it bubble and simmer for a minute or so. Reduce the heat to low and continue to cook for 6–8 minutes, stirring occasionally, until the radishes are tender all the way through and their sauce has reduced into a syrupy glaze. Taste and adjust the seasoning, if needed.

For a really lovely side dish, serve the radishes in their pan, sprinkled with sesame seeds. If I'm making a few small plates for friends, I'll serve these with garlicky yoghurt on the side, which is a nice combination.

SERVES 2, AS A SIDE

- 20g unsalted butter
- 250g breakfast radishes, greens trimmed, halved lengthways
- 1 tbsp red miso paste
- 1 tbsp brown sugar
- 100ml boiling water
- salt and freshly ground black pepper
- sesame seeds, to serve

Charred Corn, Avocado & Jalapeño Dip

I made this for friends while I was recipe testing for this book. They gobbled it up, one of them exclaiming they had never had anything like it. It's creamy and slightly spicy, with little bursts of corn. The chipotle oil adds an extra layer of flavour; smoky and spicy. I like to eat it with salted crisps, or maybe a pack of tortilla chips. You could also layer it on top of toast, if you like.

SERVES 4 AS A SNACK

olive oil
1 sweetcorn cob
400g tin cannellini beans, drained and rinsed
1 avocado, stone and skin removed
50g thick plain yoghurt
juice of 3 limes
25g pickled jalapeños
10g coriander, stalks and all
1 tsp chipotle paste
1 tsp agave (or any liquid sweetener – maple syrup, runny honey)
salt and freshly ground black pepper
a little grated lime zest, to serve

Preheat the grill to high.

Use your hands to rub a drizzle of olive oil and a pinch of salt and black pepper into the sweetcorn cob. Grill for 8–10 minutes, turning every few minutes, until lightly charred. You can do this on the BBQ, if you happen to have it on. Allow to cool, then carefully cut the sweetcorn kernels from the cob.

Combine the cannellini beans, avocado, yoghurt, most of the lime juice (saving a tablespoon for the chiplote oil), jalapeños, coriander and a good pinch of salt and black pepper in a blender. Blend until smooth and super creamy, adding a dash of water if needed, then taste and adjust the seasoning.

Combine the chipotle paste, agave, ½ tablespoon olive oil, remaining lime juice and a good pinch of salt in a small bowl. Stir well to combine, then taste and adjust the seasoning, if needed.

To serve, spread the dip out over the base of a serving plate. Spoon over the chipotle oil, and finish with the charred corn, a grating of lime zest and a good crack of black pepper. Serve with bread, crisps, crudités – whatever you wish.

GLOBE ARTICHOKE

GLOBE ARTICHOKE 101

Every time I eat a globe artichoke, I can't understand why I don't eat them more regularly. I first had one in a restaurant, prepared in almost the exact way I still like to eat them now. The magical process of peeling away each petal, dipping them in a delicious sauce and scraping off the flesh – I loved it. I guess it's similar to eating a crab or a lobster, but in vegetable form. You have to work for your dinner.

Unlike their beautiful and complex exterior, artichokes are very simple to prepare.

1. Start by topping and tailing the globe artichoke. You'll find it easiest to use a serrated knife here. Take roughly 2cm off the top, to reveal the central purple petals, and all of the stalk, so that the artichoke sits flat.

2. Next, chop a lemon in half and rub it over the cut petals of the artichoke. The artichoke will start to oxidize almost immediately at the cuts, and the lemon juice will help to slow this process down. It isn't a compulsory step and won't have an effect on the flavour of the artichoke, but it definitely makes for a prettier final product.

3. The artichoke has now been prepared. It should be able to sit flat and the purple leaves in the centre of the artichoke should be visible.

4. Place a steaming basket in a large saucepan and fill the pan with water so that it sits just below the steaming basket. Bring the pan to a boil, then place the artichoke, cut side up, into the steaming basket and cover with a lid. Reduce the heat slightly and let the artichoke steam.

5. The artichoke will take between 30 minutes and 1 hour to cook, depending on its size. Steam it for 30 minutes initially, then check on it every 5 minutes after that. Top it up every 15 minutes or so with just-boiled water, to avoid scorching your pan. You'll know when your artichoke is ready, as you should be able to easily pinch out any of the petals. If you find there is any tension when you do, allow it to steam for a little longer, until they can be picked out with ease.

DIPS FOR GLOBE ARTICHOKE

You can prepare your dip while the artichoke is steaming. Here are three of my favourites.

LEMONY, BUTTERY SAUCE: Melt 30g of salted butter and combine with 1 tbsp of lemon juice and ½ a grated garlic clove in a small bowl. Taste and add a pinch of salt, if you like.

~~~~~~~~~~~~~~~~~~~~

A CLASSIC VINAIGRETTE: Combine 2 tbsp of white wine vinegar, 1 tsp of Dijon mustard, a pinch of sugar and 2 tbsp of really good peppery extra virgin olive oil in a small bowl and whisk until smooth and combined. Season to taste with salt and black pepper.

~~~~~~~~~~~~~~~~~~~~

PESTO-ESQUE SAUCE: Combine a small handful of parsley, a small handful of basil, 10g pine nuts, 10g Parmesan, a small garlic clove and a good pinch of salt and black pepper in a small food processor (if you don't have a small one, you can use a hand blender). Blitz, pouring a few tablespoons of extra virgin olive oil slowly through the feed tube of the processor, until mostly smooth. Taste and adjust the seasoning, if needed.

HOW TO EAT YOUR ARTICHOKE

You've cooked your artichoke and prepared your dip, so now it's time to eat.

1. Use tongs to lift the globe artichoke from the pan and onto a serving plate or board. Pick each petal off the artichoke and lightly dip it into your chosen sauce. Use your teeth to scrape the fleshy part of the artichoke petal off, leaving the hard part of the petal behind to discard. Work your way around the artichoke, dipping and eating, until you reach the small purple-tipped petals.

2. Pinch and twist off the purple-tipped petals, to reveal the silky, hairy part of the artichoke called the choke. Although it wouldn't be harmful, you don't eat this part. Use a spoon to edge around the sides of the choke, where it meets the fleshy part beneath, and scrape it off to reveal the brown-grey flesh. This is the artichoke heart and is your prize!

3. Eat the artichoke heart with a spoon and a drizzle of your dipping sauce, or just with a pinch of salt. This is the part people fight over. Savour it – it's the best bit. Once you have eaten the heart, you'll be left with the hard bottom of the artichoke, which can also be discarded.

Carrot & Poppy Seed Salad

Making carrot ribbons using a speed peeler is really effective. The dressing coats the ribbons beautifully, softening them slightly so they're tender, but still keeping their crunch. I think it's a really nice dish to make for someone who doesn't like traditional salads. You can eat it on its own for a light lunch, or as a side to a quiche or a galette. It's good as part of a BBQ spread too. (See photos overleaf.)

Start by making the dressing. Combine the Dijon mustard, lemon juice, caster sugar, cumin seeds, poppy seeds, extra virgin olive oil and a good pinch of salt and black pepper in a bowl. Whisk to dissolve the sugar, then taste and adjust the seasoning, if needed.

Next, thoroughly scrub the skin of the carrots, then peel them into ribbons using a speed peeler. Any bits of carrot you are left with that you are unable to peel into ribbons, either chop them up finely and add them to the rest of the carrot, nibble on them while you continue with the recipe, or feed them to your dog. I do a mixture of all three. Combine the carrot ribbons with the chickpeas, parsley and spring onions in a mixing bowl, then pour over the dressing and mix it through. Give it a taste and add a little extra salt and/or black pepper, if you think it needs it.

It can be served straight away, but is far better after it has had time to marinate. I leave it for 20 minutes at room temperature before tucking in, giving it a stir in the middle to bring the dressing to the top. It keeps well in the fridge too.

SERVES 2, AS A MAIN

- 500g carrots (a mixture of colours, if you can get your hands on them)
- 400g jar chickpeas, drained and rinsed
- handful of parsley, leaves picked
- 2 spring onions, finely sliced
- salt and freshly ground black pepper

DRESSING

- 2 tsp Dijon mustard
- juice of ½ lemon
- 1 tsp caster sugar
- 1 tsp cumin seeds
- 2 tsp poppy seeds
- 2 tbsp extra virgin olive oil

Chilli Aioli & Thai Basil Corn

Aquafaba is the liquid from a tin or jar of beans. Its texture is perfect for whipping, similar to egg white. You'll be eating plenty of beans as you make your way through this book, so it's a nice idea to save the aquafaba and make this delicious aioli. It can be stored for up to a week in the fridge, or it will keep for much longer in the freezer. It's rather wonderful stirred through roasted vegetables, or for dipping into with tortilla chips.
(See photos overleaf.)

SERVES 4–6 GREEDY PEOPLE

olive oil
4 sweetcorn cobs
good handful of Thai basil, leaves picked
salt and freshly ground black pepper

AIOLI
100ml aquafaba (the liquid from a tin/jar of beans)
3 garlic cloves, grated
15ml lemon juice
2 generous tbsp ancho chilli paste
70ml olive oil
70ml neutral oil

Preheat the grill to medium–high.

Start by making the aioli. Combine the aquafaba, garlic, lemon juice, ancho chilli paste and a good pinch of salt in a tall jug and use a hand blender to blend until smooth. Pour the olive oil into the jug in a very slow, very thin stream, blending all the time as you do so. Do the same with the neutral oil, until you have a creamy aioli (you might not need all of the neutral oil). The aioli won't be as thick as a regular aioli at this point, but it will thicken up as it chills. Taste and adjust the seasoning, adding more lemon juice, salt, or ancho chilli paste, if you think it needs it. Refrigerate while you continue with the recipe.

Use your hands to rub a drizzle of olive oil and a sprinkle of salt and black pepper into each of the sweetcorn cobs. Grill for 8–10 minutes, turning every few minutes, until bright yellow and lightly charred. You can do this on the BBQ, if you happen to have it on.

Chop each corn cob into thirds. Combine in a mixing bowl with a few good spoonfuls of the aioli and the Thai basil leaves. Give everything a good stir, then serve up and finish with a good crack of black pepper.

A Favourite Summer Salad

It is getting increasingly hard to find great produce, but sometimes I hit the jackpot. Bright red tomatoes the size of your fist, a nectarine fragrant at arm's length. I take them home and make this. It's simple, but when you find gorgeous fruit and vegetables, it's the only way to eat them.

SERVES 2

150g ball of burrata
large handful of basil, leaves picked
1 tbsp white balsamic vinegar
1 spring onion, trimmed
½ tsp Dijon mustard
extra virgin olive oil
1 large delicious tomato (or two medium ones), sliced into wedges
1 large ripe nectarine, stoned and sliced into wedges
flaky salt and freshly ground black pepper
extra basil leaves, to serve

Before you start, take the burrata out of the fridge and leave it at room temperature for 15 minutes, to warm up a little. It's creamier this way.

Next, combine the basil leaves, white balsamic vinegar, spring onion, Dijon mustard and a good pinch of salt and black pepper in a small food processor. If you don't have a small food processor, or a smaller bowl in a regular food processor, you can combine the ingredients in a jug and use a hand blender. Blitz, adding 3–4 tablespoons of extra virgin olive oil in a thin stream through the feed tube, until you have a mostly smooth sauce which is the consistency of a dressing. Taste and adjust the seasoning, if needed.

Arrange the wedges of tomato and nectarine on a serving plate. Break over the burrata, then sprinkle with a pinch of flaky salt and a few grinds of black pepper. Drizzle with a few spoonfuls of the basil dressing, tumble over a few extra basil leaves and you're done. So simple, so fresh, so great.

A Very Simple Tomato Salad

When tomatoes are perfectly ripe, they need nothing more than a pinch of salt and a lick of olive oil to make them amazing. But when you find them slightly lacking, as I am discovering more and more often, this is how to serve them. It's still simple, but injects a little energy back into them. It's essential you serve this at room temperature. The tomatoes will thank you for it. (See photo overleaf.)

~~~~~~~~~~~~~~~~~~~

Slice the smaller tomatoes in half and the larger ones into quarters. It's quite nice to have a mixture of different sizes here, so don't worry about making them all perfectly even.

Combine the red onion, basil, garlic and a good pinch of salt and black pepper in a food processor. Blitz into a rough paste, making sure it retains some texture. You'll need to scrape the sides of the bowl a few times here.

Combine the tomatoes, onion-basil paste, extra virgin olive oil, red wine vinegar and another good pinch of salt in a mixing bowl. Give everything a good stir, then let the salad sit and marinate for at least an hour at room temperature, or up to 4, stirring it occasionally to bring the juice from the bottom to the top. If you would like to make it more than 4 hours in advance, leave it to marinate in the fridge, then bring it up to room temperature before serving.

Once the tomatoes have had time to marinate, taste and adjust the seasoning, if needed. Spoon into a serving dish, avoiding any tomato juice left at the bottom of the mixing bowl, and finish with an extra crack of black pepper and a few sprigs of fresh basil.

SERVES 4

1kg tomatoes (I like to use a mix of varieties), at room temperature
½ small red onion, peeled
10g basil, leaves picked
1 garlic clove, peeled
3 tbsp your best extra virgin olive oil
3 tbsp red wine vinegar
salt and freshly ground black pepper
a few sprigs of basil, to serve

A Peach Panzanella Salad

When juicy ripe peaches arrive in the shops, this is all I want to eat – an unexpected modern take on the classic panzanella. Fresh, vital, delightful. Don't skip the pickled red onions – their sharpness elevates the dish, making the peaches seem even sweeter than they already are.

Heat the oven to 160°C fan/350°F/gas 4.

Start by making the quick pickled onions. Combine the sliced red onion, lemon juice and a good pinch of salt in a small bowl. Use your fingers to massage them together for a minute or so, until the onions have softened and are turning pink. Set them to one side and let them macerate while you continue with the recipe.

Next, combine the bread, garlic, a good glug of olive oil and a pinch of salt on a baking tray. Use your hands to give everything a mix, then bake for 15–20 minutes, stirring halfway through, until the croûtons are crispy and golden at the edges.

For the dressing, box grate the tomato into a bowl, discarding any of the tomato skin left in your hand. Stir through the extra virgin olive oil, sherry vinegar, wholegrain mustard and a good pinch of salt and black pepper, then taste and adjust the seasoning, if needed.

Heat a griddle pan over a medium–high heat and brush with olive oil. Once hot, add the sliced peaches and griddle for 2–3 minutes on each cut side, or until grilled with dark char marks. You could also do this in a regular frying pan, if you like. You just won't get the char marks.

Combine the rocket and basil leaves in your prettiest serving dish and layer the griddled peaches, tomatoes, croûtons and quick pickled red onions on top. Break the burrata in the middle of the salad, then finish with a handful of toasted flaked almonds and a good crack of black pepper. Spoon over the dressing just before tucking in.

SERVES 2

½ red onion, very finely sliced
juice of 1 lemon
150g stale bread, torn into large chunks
1 garlic clove, grated
olive oil
2 ripe peaches, pitted and sliced into six
2 handfuls of wild rocket
handful of basil, leaves picked
2 tomatoes, roughly chopped
150g ball of burrata
salt and freshly ground black pepper
toasted flaked almonds, to serve

DRESSING

1 large tomato
3 tbsp extra virgin olive oil
1 tbsp sherry vinegar
2 tsp wholegrain mustard

Runner Bean Fattoush

This salad is a nod to fattoush, a Middle Eastern dish made traditionally with classic summer vegetables, herbs and leftover or stale pita bread, deep fried until crisp. Here I'm using runner beans, with their striking verdant pods, a sure sign of summer. Try to pick the smaller, younger runner beans. They're more tender.

In the spirit of fattoush and minimizing waste, switch out the flatbreads for any bread that needs using up. If it's too hot to turn the oven on, you could toast the flatbreads instead of baking. They won't have the same texture, but it will do the job.

Heat the oven to 160°C fan/350°F/gas 4.

Start by making the quick pickled onions. Combine the sliced red onion, lemon juice, sumac and a good pinch of salt in a small bowl. Use your fingers to massage it all together for a minute or so, until the onion has softened and is turning pink. Set it aside to macerate while you continue with the recipe.

Combine the chunks of flatbread with a good glug of olive oil and a pinch of salt and black pepper on a large baking tray. Use your hands to give everything a mix, then bake for 12–18 minutes, stirring halfway, until crisp and golden.

Combine the runner beans with a good glug of olive oil and a pinch of salt in a mixing bowl. Use your hands to evenly coat the runner beans in the oil. Now, you have two options. You can either heat up your BBQ to get it ready for cooking, or warm a griddle pan over a medium-high heat. Once hot, BBQ/griddle your beans for 3–4 minutes each side, until they are a vibrant green and have blistered and blackened in places. Depending on how large your pan is, you might need to do this in two batches. Use tongs to remove them from the pan, then chop them into 5cm pieces on the diagonal. Let them cool completely.

Meanwhile, you can make the dressing. Combine the extra virgin olive oil, lemon juice, garlic, pomegranate molasses, a pinch of salt and a good crack of black pepper in a bowl. Taste and adjust the seasoning, if needed.

Combine the runner beans, radishes, cucumbers, mint, parsley and the dressing in a mixing bowl. Add the flatbreads and gently stir them through too. Serve between bowls or on one large serving dish. Break the feta into large chunks over the top and scatter with the pickled onions. Finish with a good crack of black pepper and a few extra mint leaves, if you like.

SERVES 4

½ red onion, very finely sliced
juice of 1 lemon
1 tsp sumac
2 flatbreads, torn into chunks
olive oil
300g runner beans, hard ends trimmed
75g radishes, finely sliced
100g baby cucumbers, roughly diced
handful of mint, leaves picked and roughly chopped
handful of parsley, leaves picked and roughly chopped
200g feta
salt and freshly ground black pepper

DRESSING

2 tbsp extra virgin olive oil
juice 1 lemon
1 garlic clove, grated
1 tsp pomegranate molasses

Potatoes, Peppers & Roasted Garlic Aioli

A warm salad for for those not-quite-so-warm days in the summer months. The peppers roast up until sweet and tender and the potatoes until crisp. This recipe is worth making for the aioli alone: sweet with garlic and smoky with paprika.

SERVES 4, FOR LUNCH

1kg salad potatoes, halved
olive oil
1 garlic bulb
6 pointed red peppers, halved lengthways and deseeded
1 red chilli, deseeded and finely sliced
1 tbsp red wine vinegar
1 tbsp capers, finely chopped
small handful of parsley, leaves picked
400g jar butter beans, drained and rinsed
100g mayonnaise
2 tsp smoked paprika
small handful of flaked almonds, lightly toasted
salt and freshly ground black pepper

Preheat the oven to 180°C fan/390°F/gas 6.

Bring a large pan of salted water to the boil. Add the salad potatoes and bring the pan back to a boil. Cook for 12 minutes, then drain and let them steam dry.

Combine the parboiled potatoes, a really good glug of olive oil and a pinch of salt and pepper on a large baking tray and use your hands to give everything a good mix. Chop the head from the garlic bulb, drizzle with a little olive oil and wrap it in foil. Nestle it between the potatoes, then roast both for 40–45 minutes, stirring everything halfway through, until the potatoes are crisp and the garlic cloves are easily squeezed from their skins.

Next, combine the halved red peppers, chilli, a really good glug of olive oil and a pinch of salt and black pepper on another large baking tray. Use your hands to give everything a good mix, sitting the chilli within the curves of the red pepper. Roast alongside the potatoes for the last 30–35 minutes of their cooking time, turning them over halfway through, until tender and slightly charred at the edges.

Drizzle the roasted red peppers with red wine vinegar and add the capers, parsley and butter beans to their tray. Give everything a good mix.

To make the aioli, squeeze out the flesh of the roasted garlic and combine with the mayonnaise, smoked paprika and a good grind of black pepper. Taste and add a pinch of salt, if you think it needs it.

Layer the marinated red peppers, butter beans and crispy potatoes in a serving dish or between plates. Drizzle over or serve with the aioli, sprinkle with the toasted flaked almonds and finish with a good crack of black pepper. Use a roasted potato to scrape up any leftover aioli from its bowl and pop it straight into your mouth. You won't want to waste it.

Crispy Rice, Smashed Cucumbers & Black Bean Salad

I have a real affinity with Chinese smacked cucumber salads. There is a really good recipe in Verna Gao's *Have You Eaten?*, which is where I first discovered them. I'll eat them mostly as a side for sushi bowls, noodles and stir-fries. But in this recipe, my beloved smacked cucumbers become a meal on their own. The reason for smacking (or smashing) the cucumbers is to break down their fibres, forcing little cuts and cracks, creating a more porous surface to suck up all that glorious dressing. I find it very satisfying to do, too.

This is a lovely way to use up leftover rice. If making from scratch, cook 175g of rice according to the packet instructions. Allow it to cool completely, then continue as normal.

Preheat the oven to 200°C fan/425°F/gas 7.

Start by preparing the crispy rice. Combine your cooked rice, the miso mixture, cornflour and a good drizzle of neutral oil in a mixing bowl. Use your hands to give everything a mix, making sure the rice is evenly coated, then pour out onto a baking tray and spread into an even layer. Bake for 20–25 minutes, gently stirring everything halfway through (trying not to break up any lumps that have formed), until the rice is crisp on the edges but a still a little chewy in the middle. Let it cool completely.

Meanwhile, place the cucumber on a chopping board and use a rolling pin, or just your fist, to bash up and down its whole length and on every side, not so hard that it cracks into two, but hard enough so that small cracks appear on its surface. Slice it lengthways down the middle, then chop it into 2.5cm diagonal chunks.

Combine the caster sugar, sesame oil, soy sauce, rice vinegar, garlic, chilli crisp, spring onions, sesame seeds and coriander in a mixing bowl. Stir well to dissolve the sugar, then taste and add a pinch of salt, if you think it needs it. Stir the chopped cucumber through the dressing, then set it aside to sit and macerate while you wait for the rice to cool.

Stir the cooled rice and black beans through the cucumber and its dressing. Taste and adjust the seasoning, if needed, then divide the salad between bowls. Serve with a little extra coriander on the top, or an extra drizzle of chilli crisp, if you like things spicy.

SERVES 2, GENEROUSLY

450g cooked jasmine rice
1 tbsp miso paste, mixed with 1 tbsp water
1 tsp cornflour
neutral oil
1 large cucumber
1 tsp caster sugar
1 tsp sesame oil
1½ tbsp light soy sauce
1 tbsp rice vinegar
2 garlic cloves, grated
1 tsp chilli crisp oil, plus extra for serving (optional)
2 spring onions, finely sliced
2 tsp sesame seeds (whatever you have – white or black)
small handful of coriander, leaves picked, plus extra to serve
400g jar black beans, drained and rinsed
salt

Aubergine Schnitzel, Cucumber Salad

I'm not a big fan of fruit or vegetables disguising themselves as traditional meat dishes. Cauliflower steaks for example. Or even worse, watermelon steaks. However, to contradict myself: here is my schnitzel made from aubergine. But really, the title is just my way of describing that it is breadcrumbed. Think of it as crispy, crunchy, delicious aubergine. This cucumber salad is my take on a German dish called gurkensalat. Together they make a lovely lunch. If you fancy something a bit different, try them both in a warm ciabatta. Gorgeous. (See photo overleaf.)

Preheat the grill to high.

Rub the aubergines all over with a little neutral oil. Grill for 15–20 minutes, turning them every 5 minutes or so, until the skin has charred and the flesh inside is soft and squidgy. You could also burn the aubergine over the flame of a gas hob, until the skin has blackened and the flesh is tender (don't rub them with oil if choosing this method). Once the aubergines are cool enough to touch, gently peel off the charred skin, trying not to bring any of the flesh along with it and keeping the stem attached.

To make the cucumber salad, combine the cucumber and a good pinch of salt in a sieve, set either over a bowl, or in the sink. Use your hands to massage the salt into the cucumber for a few minutes, softening it as you do so. Set aside for 15 minutes, letting the water from the cucumber drain away.

Combine the soured cream, garlic, white wine vinegar, sugar, cornichons, dill and a good pinch of salt and black pepper in a bowl and stir well. Once your cucumber has rested, use your hands to squeeze out any excess water and stir it through the dressing. Taste and adjust the seasoning, if needed.

Use a fork to gently flatten the aubergines, still keeping their stalks intact, then sprinkle both sides with a little pinch of salt. Combine the milk, cornflour and a pinch of salt in a shallow bowl and whisk until smooth. Tip the flour onto a plate and season with a pinch of salt and black pepper. Pour the breadcrumbs onto another plate and you are ready to go.

Recipe continues overleaf

SERVES 2

2 aubergines
neutral oil
100ml milk
1 tbsp cornflour
50g plain flour
100g panko breadcrumbs
salt and freshly ground black pepper

CUCUMBER SALAD

½ cucumber, very finely sliced
75ml soured cream
1 small garlic clove, grated
1 tsp white wine vinegar
pinch of sugar
4 cornichons, finely sliced
small handful of dill, leaves picked and finely chopped

Heat a large frying pan over a medium heat and add enough oil to coat the bottom. When hot, take each flattened aubergine and dip it first in the flour, turning it over to thoroughly coat both sides. Then into the milk mixture, then into the breadcrumbs, making sure both sides are generously coated and covered. When the oil is hot, fry the aubergines for 3–4 minutes undisturbed on each side, until they are crisp and deeply golden. If they are browning much quicker than this, reduce the heat slightly. Try not to move them too much; let them do their thing. Remove them from the oil and onto a few sheets of kitchen towel, to soak up any excess grease.

Serve the aubergine between plates and top with a generous portion of the cucumber salad. Finish with a pinch of flaky salt, a good crack of black pepper and maybe a few extra sprigs of dill, if you like.

Fennel, Tomato & Salsa Verde Traybake

SERVES 2

2 fennel bulbs, quartered and fronds saved for garnish
200g baby potatoes, halved
250g medium-sized tomatoes, halved
juice of 1 lemon
5 sprigs of thyme
1 tsp caster sugar
olive oil
400g jar butter beans, drained and rinsed
salt and freshly ground black pepper

SALSA VERDE

1 large garlic clove, minced
30g parsley, hard stalks trimmed and leaves finely chopped
30g basil, hard stalks trimmed and leaves finely chopped
15g mint, leaves picked and finely chopped
2 tbsp capers, finely chopped
2 tsp Dijon mustard
3 tbsp red wine vinegar
extra virgin olive oil

Fennel is often unfairly dismissed. Although I enjoy it, I understand that its strong aniseed flavour isn't everyone's favourite. There are ways to prepare fennel that soften its aniseed flavour and bring out its earthy natural sweetness, like braising or roasting. If you have overlooked fennel in the past, I urge you to try it roasted, as it is in this recipe. I hope it will be a revelation.

This recipe is inspired by a tray-baked salad I found in *How To Eat A Peach* by Diana Henry. A fabulous book for those who like hosting. In fact, it's where I first came across the concept of a tray-baked salad in general. Another revelation.

You'll most probably have leftover salsa verde here; what a joy! Eat it with everything and anything. It's particularly nice on your breakfast scrambled eggs.

Preheat the oven to 200°C fan/425°F/gas 7.

Combine the fennel, potatoes, tomatoes, lemon juice, thyme and sugar with a good glug of olive oil and a generous pinch of salt and black pepper in a baking dish. Use your hands to give everything a mix, then cover the dish with foil and roast for 30 minutes. Remove the foil and return the dish to the oven for a further 25–35 minutes, stirring once halfway through, until the potatoes are crisp and the fennel is tender all the way through.

Meanwhile, make the salsa verde. Combine the garlic, parsley, basil, mint, capers, Dijon mustard, red wine vinegar and a big pinch of salt and black pepper in a small bowl. Add just enough extra virgin olive oil to cover it, then give everything a good stir (you could also make this in a food processor, but it's nice when it has some texture, so make sure you don't blend it until completely smooth). Taste and adjust the seasoning, adding more vinegar, salt, or anything you think it may need.

Add the butter beans and a good few spoonfuls of the salsa verde (any leftovers will keep for a week in the fridge) to the tray with the roasted vegetables and stir well to combine. Serve between plates and finish with an extra drizzle of the salsa verde, any fronds you managed to save from the fennel bulbs and a good crack of black pepper.

Aubergines & Golden Sauce

It may seem daunting to make your own curry paste, but it is actually much easier than you'd think. It's just a question of shoving everything in a food processor and you're set. There is always a time and a place for convenience food in my opinion, and for pre-made curry paste, too. But do try making it yourself when you can. The aroma that fills the air is worth it alone.

This recipe calls for coconut cream, which is thicker and richer than coconut milk, just as double cream is thicker and richer than regular milk. It's different from creamed coconut, however, which I use in my Beetroot Dhal on page 172. Creamed coconut comes in a solid block and is made from the flesh of the coconut without any added water. They are all interchangeable; you'll just need to adjust the quantities of any other liquids in the recipe accordingly. There is more information about how to do this in my Cook's Note on page 14.

SERVES 4

3 aubergines, cubed
neutral oil
1 tsp caster sugar
500ml vegetable stock
160ml coconut cream
salt and freshly ground black pepper

CURRY PASTE
1 tsp cumin seeds
2 tsp coriander seeds
4 spring onions, trimmed and greens/whites separated
5 garlic cloves, peeled
large thumb-sized piece of ginger (don't bother peeling it)
2 red chillies, deseeded
1 tbsp ground turmeric
1 tbsp mild curry powder
1 stick lemongrass (fresh is best, but dried if not)
4 kaffir lime leaves

TO SERVE
boiled rice
salted roasted cashew nuts (or salt and pepper cashews if you can find them)
handful of coriander leaves

Preheat the oven to 160°C fan/350°F/gas 4.

Combine the aubergine with a good glug of neutral oil and a pinch of salt and black pepper on a large baking tray, or, between two smaller ones. Use your hands to give everything a mix, then roast for 25–30 minutes, stirring once halfway through, until they are golden brown at the edge and tender in the middle.

Meanwhile, make your curry paste. Heat a small dry frying pan over a low–medium heat. Once hot, add the cumin and coriander seeds and toast for a minute or two, stirring frequently, until they darken slightly and release their fragrance. Watch them carefully, as they can turn from browned to burnt in a matter of seconds. Remove from the heat and let them cool.

Combine the toasted cumin and coriander seeds, the whites of the spring onions, garlic, ginger, red chillies, turmeric, curry powder, lemongrass, kaffir lime leaves and a good pinch of salt in a food processor. Blitz the mixture, scraping the sides of the bowl a few times if needed, until you have a smooth paste.

If your food processor requires a little dash of water to help it along, that's fine. You just want to try and get the paste as smooth as possible.

Next, heat a good glug of neutral oil in a large pan over a medium heat. Once hot, add the curry paste and cook for 3–4 minutes, stirring constantly, until it fills the room with its perfume and has darkened in colour. Add the sugar, vegetable stock, coconut cream and a good pinch of salt and black pepper, then bring everything to a simmer. Lower the heat slightly and cook for 6–8 minutes, stirring regularly, until the sauce has reduced a little, but is still brothy. Add the roasted aubergine and simmer for a further 5–6 minutes, to infuse the aubergine with the gorgeous sauce. Taste and adjust the seasoning, if needed.

Spoon freshly boiled rice between shallow bowls and ladle the aubergine and golden sauce on top, letting the aubergine balance on top of the rice and the sauce pool around the edges. Finish with a handful of salt and pepper cashews, finely sliced greens of the spring onions, coriander and a few good grinds of black pepper.

Tomato Curry, Crispy Tofu, Rice

A curry, for summer.

This tofu crumb is great if you are new to tofu, or don't think it's your thing. It's crispy and crunchy, adding a satisfying bite to the soft, sweet tomatoes.

SERVES 4

1½ tsp black mustard seeds
1 tsp cumin seeds
1½ tsp coriander seeds
neutral oil
1 large onion (or 2 smaller ones), finely sliced
12 dried curry leaves
5 garlic cloves, minced
1 red chilli, deseeded and finely sliced
1kg tomatoes (I use a mixture of varieties), large ones quartered, small ones halved
200ml coconut milk
2 tsp brown sugar
2 tsp white wine vinegar
salt and freshly ground black pepper
rice, to serve

TOFU CRUMB
280g extra-firm tofu
1 tbsp cornflour
1 tsp garam masala
½ tsp ground cumin
small handful fresh coriander, leaves picked and very finely chopped
¼ red onion, sliced very finely with a mandoline

Preheat the oven to 180°C fan/390°F/gas 6.

Heat your largest high-sided frying pan over a low–medium heat. Once hot, add the black mustard seeds, cumin seeds and coriander seeds and toast for a minute or two, until they release their fragrance and begin to brown. Watch them carefully here, as they can burn quickly. Grind into a powder in a pestle and mortar, then set them aside for later.

Next, heat a really good glug of oil in the same pan set over a medium heat. Once hot, add the onion and a pinch of salt and fry for 8–10 minutes, stirring regularly, until soft and golden. Add the ground spices, curry leaves, garlic and chilli and fry for a further 2–3 minutes, until the spices release their fragrance.

Add the tomatoes, coconut milk, brown sugar and a good pinch of salt to the pan. Give everything a good stir and bring to a gentle simmer. Reduce the heat to low and cook, undisturbed, for 40–45 minutes, or until most of the liquid in the pan has evaporated and the tomatoes are thick and jammy. Stir through the white wine vinegar and a good crack of black pepper, then taste and adjust the seasoning, if needed.

Meanwhile, you can make the tofu crumb. Pat the tofu dry with a tea towel, to remove any excess liquid. Pulse in a food processor into a fine crumble, then combine with the cornflour, garam masala, cumin and a good pinch of salt and black pepper in a mixing bowl. Drizzle liberally with oil and use your hands to give everything a good mix. Pour out onto a large baking tray and bake for 20–25 minutes, stirring halfway through, until the tofu is golden brown and crispy. Stir through the coriander, red onion and a good crack of black pepper, then taste and adjust the seasoning, if needed.

Serve the rice between bowls and spoon over the tomato curry. Sprinkle the tofu crumb generously on top, then dig in. It's a fork-only kind of dish. My favourite.

Burnt Aubergine & Chimichurri Pasta

BBQs are for so much more than just sausages and burgers. Whenever I'm offered the chance to use mine during the summer months, I take it. There is a magic imparted to vegetables by the coals and flames – here the aubergine skins blacken and blister, the flesh softening into a smoky, silky richness. The butter and pasta water emulsify the aubergine into a velvety sauce, clinging in the ridges of the rigatoni; the chimichurri crumb finishing it off with crunch, tang and heat.

Heat the oven to 180°C fan/390°F/gas 6 and preheat your BBQ to get it ready for cooking.

Place the aubergines on the BBQ. Cook them for 10–20 minutes (depending on how hot your BBQ is), turning occasionally, until the skin is a deep, rich black all over (shut the lid of the BBQ between turning, to help them along). If you don't want to use the BBQ, you can use tongs to burn the aubergines over the flame of a gas stove instead. Set aside until cool enough to touch.

Chop the aubergines in half lengthways and use a fork to scrape the flesh from the skin. Discard the blackened skin, then mash the aubergine flesh into a rough paste.

Meanwhile, to make the crumb, combine the sourdough and a pinch of salt on a baking tray. Drizzle with a glug of olive oil, then give everything a good mix and bake for 12–15 minutes, or until crisp all the way through and golden at the edges. Transfer into a food processor along with the parsley, chilli, oregano and a good crack of black pepper and whizz into a fine crumb. Taste and adjust the seasoning, if needed.

Cook the pasta in salted water according to the packet instructions.

Warm a good glug of olive oil in a large frying pan over a medium heat. Once hot, add the garlic and fry for a minute or so, just to soften. Add the lemon zest and aubergine flesh and stir well to combine. Add the butter, a ladleful of pasta water and a few good cracks of black pepper and stir until the butter has melted and the sauce has emulsified. Taste and adjust the seasoning, if needed, then keep warm over a low heat.

Spoon the pasta into the sauce and stir well. If the sauce is too thick to cover all the pasta, add a little more pasta water and stir again, until glossy. Divide the pasta between bowls and serve topped generously with the sourdough crumb, another grating of lemon zest and a good crack of black pepper.

SERVES 4

- 3 aubergines
- olive oil
- 400g pasta of choice (I like rigatoni for this)
- 4 garlic cloves, minced
- zest of 1 lemon, plus extra to serve
- 75g salted butter
- salt and freshly ground black pepper

SOURDOUGH CRUMB

- 100g stale sourdough bread, chopped into chunks
- 20g parsley, stalks and all
- 1 red chilli, deseeded and sliced
- 1 tsp dried oregano

Really Easy Tomato & Gnocchi Bake

This is nothing particularly glamorous, but when I'm stuck for time or have no inspiration for what to eat, I'll have this. The roasted tomatoes melt into a jammy sauce as you stir everything together, and the gnocchi roasts to a crisp and chewy texture. It's a simple recipe, so it helps if you treat yourself to good ingredients: sweet juicy tomatoes and great olive oil.

SERVES 2

400g fresh potato gnocchi
500g small ripe tomatoes
3 garlic cloves, minced
1 sprig of rosemary, leaves picked and roughly chopped
olive oil
handful of basil, leaves picked
salt and freshly ground black pepper
grated Parmesan, to serve

Preheat the oven to 200°C fan/425°F/gas 7.

Combine the gnocchi, tomatoes, garlic, rosemary and a really good pinch of salt and black pepper on a baking tray. Drizzle everything with a glug of olive oil, then stir to coat and combine.

Bake for 25–30 minutes, stirring halfway through, until the gnocchi is crisp and the tomatoes are soft.

Scatter the tray with half of the basil, then give everything a good mix. Divide the gnocchi between two bowls and garnish with the remaining basil, a good few cracks of pepper and a grating of Parmesan.

Aubergine Stew, Whipped Tahini Sauce

Just after the Covid lockdown, I set up my own cookery school. The concept was slightly different to most – yes, it taught people how to cook, but the small intimate classes meant we could chat, get to know one another and make new connections – something we hadn't had the chance to do for so long. At the end of the class, we would all sit down together and enjoy the fruits of our labour. They were special evenings.

The menu changed with the seasons and with my mood. My aubergine stew, an appreciation of the Lebanese dish maghmour, made a regular appearance in the summer months and was a favourite with the class. The fresh tomatoes break down into a rich, luscious sauce. It's glorious.

SERVES 4, GENEROUSLY

4 aubergines, cubed
extra virgin olive oil
1 large onion, finely chopped
5 garlic cloves, finely chopped
2 tsp ground mixed spice
1 tsp ground cinnamon
800g tomatoes, roughly chopped
2 tsp caster sugar
700g jar chickpeas, drained and rinsed
juice of ½ lemon
salt and freshly ground black pepper
handful of chopped parsley, to serve

WHIPPED TAHINI SAUCE
125g tahini
juice of ½ lemon
1 tsp olive oil
4 tbsp plain yoghurt

Preheat the oven to 180°C fan/390°F/gas 6.

Combine the cubed aubergine, a good glug of olive oil and a generous pinch of salt in a mixing bowl. Use your hands to give everything a good mix, then arrange between two baking trays and roast for 20–25 minutes, mixing once halfway through, until soft and turning golden.

Meanwhile, heat a good glug of olive oil in a large ovenproof pot over a medium heat. Once hot, add the onion and a pinch of salt and fry for 6–8 minutes, until soft and translucent. Add the garlic, mixed spice and cinnamon and fry for a further minute or so, until the spices release their fragrance. Next, add the tomatoes, sugar, 400ml water, a good pinch of salt and a few cracks of black pepper. Stir well, then bring to the boil. Reduce the heat to a simmer and cook for 10 minutes, stirring regularly, until the tomatoes have started to break down.

Stir through the chickpeas and roasted aubergine, then cover the pan with a lid. Transfer the whole pot to the oven and bake for 1 hour 45 minutes–2 hours, or until the maghmour is thick and rich. Squeeze in the lemon juice and stir as you watch the tomatoes transform into a gorgeous sauce. Taste and adjust the seasoning, if needed.

Meanwhile, to make the whipped tahini sauce, combine the tahini, lemon juice, olive oil, yoghurt and a good pinch of salt in a mixing bowl. Add 75ml of cold water and whisk well to combine, until creamy and lighter in colour. Taste and adjust the seasoning, if needed.

Serve the stew, whipped tahini and a pot of chopped parsley on the table. Give everyone a bowl and let them dig in.

Spanakopíta Beans

Beans, inspired by the flavours of a spanakopita – spinach, feta, lemon, dill, parsley, nutmeg. It's super green goodness, with enough sauce that you can mop up the leftovers with a nice bit of crusty bread. I love it for brunch or lunch.

SERVES 2–3

olive oil
4 spring onions, finely sliced
3 garlic cloves, minced
1 tsp dried mint
¼ tsp freshly grated nutmeg
700g jar butter beans
250g baby spinach, washed
10g dill, leaves picked, plus extra to serve
10g parsley, stalks and all
zest and juice of 1 lemon
100g feta
salt and freshly ground black pepper

TO SERVE
a little grated lemon zest
crusty bread

Heat a good glug of olive oil in a large pan over a medium heat. Once hot, add the spring onions, garlic and a pinch of salt and fry, stirring frequently, for 2–3 minutes, until the whites of the spring onions are turning translucent. Add the dried mint and nutmeg and stir them through.

Add the beans, with their liquid, and stir well to combine. Bring the pan to a gentle simmer, then reduce the heat to low and cook for 5–6 minutes, stirring regularly, until the beans are ultra tender and their liquid has reduced almost completely.

Meanwhile, combine the spinach, dill and parsley in a large colander in the sink. Pour a kettle of freshly boiled water over the greens to wilt them, then run under cold water until cool. Give them a good shake to help drain the water (do not squeeze them), then combine with the lemon zest and juice, 40ml of water and a good pinch of salt. Blend until smooth and velvety.

Stir the spinach paste through the beans. Taste and adjust the seasoning, if needed, then remove the pan from the heat. Crumble the feta over the top and let it melt into the beans. Finish with a few extra sprigs of dill, a grating of lemon zest and a good crack of black pepper. Eat with lots of crusty bread.

Zhoug & Smoky Aubergine Sandwiches

I love griddling aubergines; the smoky flesh collapsing beneath their skin. I've paired them with my take on zhoug, an addictive spicy green Yemeni sauce. It's a very impressive sandwich.

You're likely to end up with leftover zhoug, which is a fantastic problem to have. Eat it with eggs, flatbreads, hummus or with a spoon.

Start by making the zhoug. Heat a dry frying pan over a low-medium heat and add the cumin and cardamom seeds. Toast for a minute or so, until they release their fragrance and begin to brown. Watch them carefully here, as they can burn quickly. Grind into a powder in a pestle and mortar and combine with the chopped coriander, green chillies, garlic, lemon juice and a good pinch of salt and black pepper in a small bowl. Pour over just enough extra virgin olive oil to cover the mixture and stir well (you could also make this in a food processor, but it's nice when it has some texture, so don't over-blend it). Taste and adjust the seasoning, if needed.

To make the tahini yoghurt, combine the tahini, lemon juice, maple syrup, yoghurt, 1 teaspoon extra virgin olive oil, 25ml water and a good pinch of salt in a small bowl. Whisk until thick and creamy, then taste and adjust the seasoning, if needed. Refrigerate until ready to serve.

Next, heat a griddle pan over a medium-high heat. Rub the aubergines with olive oil and griddle for 10–15 minutes, turning occasionally, until the skin has charred and the flesh is tender. You could also do this under the grill or on the BBQ, if you have it on.

Once the aubergines are cool enough to touch, scrape off the charred skin with your fingers and discard, then pull the flesh apart with two forks. Combine the pulled aubergine flesh with a few spoonfuls of the zhoug in a mixing bowl and stir well to combine.

To serve, warm or toast your ciabatta and slice in half. Spread generously with the tahini yoghurt, then spoon the zhoug aubergine on top. Finish with an extra spoonful of the zhoug and a crack of black pepper. Press on the top ciabatta half, chop into two and enjoy while still warm. You might want a bib.

MAKES 2 GENEROUS SANDWICHES

2 aubergines
extra virgin olive oil
1 large ciabatta
salt and freshly ground black pepper

ZHOUG
1 tsp cumin seeds
½ tsp cardamom seeds, measured after removing from pods
30g coriander, stalks and all, finely chopped
2 green chillies, deseeded and finely chopped
2 garlic cloves, finely chopped
juice of 1 lemon

TAHINI YOGHURT
125g tahini
juice of ½ lemon
1 tbsp maple syrup
5 tbsp plain yoghurt

Creamed Corn Cannellini Beans

This dish is so simple, with very few ingredients, too. I would suggest using the best-quality beans and bread you can find – it really will make all the difference.

Melt the butter in a large heavy-bottomed pan over a medium heat. Add the spring onions and fry for 2–3 minutes, stirring frequently, until they are softened and turning translucent.

Add the corn kernels and stir them through the butter. Pour in 100ml of water and season with a good pinch of salt. Stir well, then bring everything to a simmer. Reduce the heat slightly and cook for 3–4 minutes, stirring regularly, until the corn is bright yellow and tender.

Meanwhile, use your hands to rub a drizzle of olive oil and a sprinkle of salt and black pepper into the third sweetcorn cob. Grill for 8–10 minutes, turning every few minutes, until lightly charred. Carefully cut the sweetcorn kernels from their cob and set aside.

Add the cream to the pan, stir well to combine and remove from the heat. Ladle half of the mixture into a high-powered blender and blend until smooth and velvety. Pour the mixture back into the pan, along with the beans, and stir well to combine.

Return the pan to a medium heat and bring everything to a gentle simmer. Cook for a further 2–3 minutes, or until the beans have warmed through and the sauce has reduced a little. Season to taste with salt and lots of black pepper.

Serve the beans sprinkled with smoked paprika, the charred corn and extra spring onion. Finish with a good crack of black pepper and eat with lots of crusty bread.

SERVES 2, WITH LEFTOVERS

- 75g unsalted butter
- 3 spring onions, finely sliced, plus extra to serve
- 3 sweetcorn cobs, kernels cut from two and one left whole
- olive oil
- 150ml single cream
- 700g jar cannellini beans, drained and rinsed
- salt and freshly ground black pepper

TO SERVE
- smoked paprika
- really nice crusty bread

Bean Confit

SERVES 1 IF YOU'RE HUNGRY,
2 IF YOU'RE NOT

400g jar cannellini beans,
   drained and rinsed
4 garlic cloves, peeled
1 red chilli, finely chopped
small handful of basil, leaves
   picked and finely chopped
5 baby tomatoes, halved
your best extra virgin olive oil
salt and freshly ground black
   pepper

TO SERVE
handful of basil leaves
crusty toast

This is a simple dish with simple ingredients, yet it excites me every time I make it. To confit as a cooking term (literally, to preserve, in French) is cooking food in fat or oil, locking in moisture and creating rich flavour.

It is a dish of few ingredients, so we want to use great ones. Good quality beans, lovely ripe tomatoes and the best extra virgin olive oil you have in the house. The chilli adds a lovely warmth, but for those with an aversion to spice, you can of course skip it. Or, add extra, for the spice-lovers.

Preheat the oven to 180°C fan/390°F/gas 6.

Combine the cannellini beans, garlic, red chilli, basil, baby tomatoes and a really good pinch of salt and black pepper in a small baking dish. Your dish needs to be small enough for the mixture to almost reach the top. A ceramic tapas dish is perfect.

Pour over enough extra virgin olive oil to almost submerge the mixture, leaving a few of the beans naked at the top. Bake for 30–35 minutes, until the garlic is tender, the top is crispy and the oil is bubbling.

Serve the bean confit in its dish, with a little extra basil if you like. Finish with a crack of black pepper and eat with lots of crusty toast, dipping and dousing it in the delicious oil.

Cold Peanut Noodles & Charred Lettuce

I first discovered the joys of cold noodles from Verna Gao and her book *Have You Eaten?* They are chewy and delightfully refreshing. Addictive, in fact. I believe Verna is also responsible for the huge amount of peanut butter consumed in my house.

I find my knife-cut noodles (also known as Taiwanese-style sliced noodles or flower petal noodles) in my local Asian supermarket, where I love browsing the aisles. The big supermarkets in my area don't seem to stock them, but you might have more luck where you live. If you're really stuck, they can easily be found online and are worth holding out for.

SERVES 2

1 small garlic clove, grated
½ thumb-sized piece of ginger, grated
1½ tbsp rice vinegar
200g dried knife-cut ribbon noodles
2 tbsp light soy sauce
3½ tbsp smooth peanut butter
1½ tbsp sesame oil
salt

CHARRED LETTUCE
sesame oil
2 little gem lettuces, washed, dried and halved lengthways

TO SERVE
black sesame seeds
chilli crisp oil

Combine the grated garlic, ginger and rice vinegar in a mixing bowl. Stir well, then set aside and let them macerate while you continue with the recipe.

Cook the noodles in salted boiling water according to the packet instructions. Drain, then run under cold water until cool.

Heat a griddle pan over a high heat and brush with sesame oil. Once hot, griddle the lettuces, cut side down, for a minute or so, pressing them down until they are grilled with dark char marks, but still crisp on top. You could also do this in a regular frying pan. You just won't get the char marks.

Add the soy sauce, peanut butter, sesame oil and 2½ tablespoons of cold water to the macerated garlic and ginger and whisk until smooth and creamy. Taste and add a pinch of salt, if you think it needs it. Gently stir through the noodles, to coat them in the sauce. They should be glossy. If they aren't, add a dash more water.

Twist the noodles into bowls and top with the charred lettuce. Sprinkle with a pinch of black sesame seeds and drizzle with a spoonful or two of chilli crisp, if you like spice.

Slow-Cooked Courgette Tagliatelle

SERVES 2

olive oil
500g courgettes, very finely sliced (this is much easier if you use a mandoline)
3 garlic cloves, minced
225g tagliatelle (or any other long pasta shape – spaghetti, bucatini, etc.)
juice of ½ lemon
2 heaped tbsp full-fat cream cheese
good handful of basil, leaves picked and finely chopped
salt and freshly ground black pepper

TO SERVE

toasted pine nuts
a little grated lemon zest
handful of basil leaves

Something magical happens when you slow-cook courgettes. They crumple and fold into a rich, velvety sauce. It needs patience, but very little skill. Treat this as you would a risotto; take your time. Stick on some music, pour yourself a drink and relax into the process.

Heat a really good glug of olive oil in a large frying pan over a low heat. Once hot, add the sliced courgettes and a pinch of salt and fry gently for 20 minutes, stirring regularly, until they begin to break down and fall apart. Add the garlic and fry for a further 15–20 minutes, stirring regularly and adding a touch more olive oil if the pan gets too dry, until the courgettes have collapsed and are lightly golden.

Meanwhile, cook the tagliatelle in well-salted water according to the packet instructions, until al dente.

Stir the lemon juice, cream cheese, basil and a good pinch of salt and black pepper through the courgettes. Lift the pasta from its pan and into the sauce with a pair of tongs, bringing some of the pasta water along with it. Stir well to combine, adding a ladleful, or two, of pasta water to loosen the courgettes into a silky sauce. Taste and adjust the seasoning, if needed.

Twist the pasta into bowls and finish with a few toasted pine nuts, a grating of lemon zest, a few sprigs of basil and as much black pepper as you like.

Fennel & Sausage Pappardelle

This is the least classically summery recipe in this chapter, because it has a silky, luscious sauce associated more with the winter months. But the summer weather is unpredictable in the UK and in many other countries in the world, so I wanted to give you a summer pasta for days it feels like winter.

Fennel is in season between July and October in the UK, so this recipe will carry over to autumn quite nicely. Its elegant fronds add an extra whisper of aniseed, to finish.

You could add some breadcrumbs here too, if you like a little crunch. Personally, I serve the dish as written, highlighting its opulence, but the Chilli Pangrattato recipe from page 54 would be a nice addition, if you like.

SERVES 4

olive oil
400g sausages (if vegetarian, make sure they are the type with the casing)
2 fennel bulbs, very finely sliced with a mandoline and fennel fronds reserved
2 banana shallots, finely sliced
3 garlic cloves, minced
1 red chilli, deseeded and finely chopped
1 tsp fennel seeds
100ml white wine
200ml vegetable stock
400g pappardelle
225g mascarpone
50g Parmesan, finely grated
salt and freshly ground black pepper
extra virgin olive oil, to serve

Heat a good glug of oil in a large frying pan over medium heat. Use a sharp knife to slice down the side of each sausage and peel off its casing. Use your fingers to pull off small sections of the sausage meat and drop them in the oil, creating little uneven meatballs. Fry the sausage meat for 6–8 minutes, stirring occasionally, until glistening and golden and cooked all the way through. Use a slotted spoon to remove the sausage meat from the oil and into a bowl lined with kitchen towel, to soak up any excess grease, leaving all the fat behind in the pan.

Deglaze the pan with a little water, scraping all the yummy crispy bits off the bottom. Add the fennel, shallots and a pinch of salt and stir to coat them the oil and the crispy bits. Reduce the heat to low and cook for 25–30 minutes, stirring regularly, until the fennel is soft, golden and a little caramelized. Add the garlic, red chilli and fennel seeds and fry for a further 4–5 minutes, just to soften.

Increase the heat to medium. Pour in the white wine and allow to simmer and bubble for minute or so, until almost evaporated. Add the vegetable stock and a good pinch of salt, then bring the pan to a gentle simmer and cook for 2–3 minutes, stirring frequently, to slightly reduce the vegetable stock.

Next, cook your pappardelle in salted water, according to the packet instructions.

Stir the mascarpone and Parmesan through the fennel, to melt them into a sauce. Add the sausage meat, stir well, then keep the sauce warm over a very low heat, while you wait for your pasta.

Lift the pappardelle from its pan and into the sauce with a pair of tongs, bringing some of the pasta water along with it. Stir well to combine, adding a ladleful, or two, of pasta water to loosen the sauce, if needed. It should be glossy and silky and coat the pappardelle with ease. Taste and adjust the seasoning, if needed.

Twist into bowls and finish with a swirl of your best olive oil, any fennel fronds you managed to keep back and a good crack of black pepper.

A Very Herby Noodle Soup

I have been inspired by a Persian noodle soup called ash reshteh here. It's a celebration dish, served in the lead-up to the Persian New Year. My version is far from traditional, rather a nod in appreciation of the original dish, using ingredients more readily available in my local area.

This makes a big pot full. Party-sized, if you like. You could make it on a smaller scale, but you'll end up with leftover beans, which isn't the end of the world. I prefer to make it in full scale, then freeze the leftovers in portions. Skip the crispy onions if you do this though – just add some fresh spring onion on top, or serve it without.

SERVES 6, BUT FREEZES WELL

100g coriander, hard stalks removed
100g parsley, hard stalks removed
100g dill, hard stalks removed
250g baby spinach
neutral oil
8 spring onions, finely sliced
2 garlic cloves, minced
½ tsp ground turmeric
400g jar chickpeas, drained and rinsed
400g jar kidney beans, drained and rinsed
400g tin green lentils, drained and rinsed
1.5 litres good quality vegetable stock
150g linguine
2 tbsp soured cream, plus extra to serve
salt and freshly ground black pepper

CRISPY SPRING ONIONS
4 spring onions, sliced into thin lengths
2 tbsp cornflour

Combine the coriander, parsley, dill and spinach in a food processor and blitz until finely chopped. Depending on how large your food processor is, you might not be able to fit everything in straight away. Start with less and add more as you blitz. You'll end up with something like a rough paste. Set it aside for later.

Heat a good glug of neutral oil in your largest pan over a medium heat. Once hot, fry the spring onions and a pinch of salt for 4–5 minutes, until the whites of the spring onions are turning translucent. Add the garlic and turmeric and fry for a further minute or so, just to soften. Stir through the chickpeas, kidney beans and lentils to coat them in the oil.

Pour the stock into the pan and stir well. Bring the pan to a boil, then reduce the heat to low and cover with a lid. Cook for 20–25 minutes, stirring occasionally, until the stock has reduced and the beans and lentils are really tender. Add the finely chopped herbs and spinach and a good pinch of salt and cook, uncovered this time, for a further 5 minutes, letting them melt into the soup.

Meanwhile, make the crispy spring onions. Combine the lengths of spring onion, cornflour and a pinch of salt in a mixing bowl and stir well to coat. Heat roughly 2cm of neutral oil in a small pan set over a medium heat. When hot, fry the onion in two batches for about 3 minutes, until golden and crispy. Use a slotted spoon to remove them from the oil and onto sheets of kitchen towel, to soak up any excess grease.

Recipe continues overleaf

Snap the linguine in two and add it to the soup pan. Increase the heat to medium and cook for a further 10–15 minutes, stirring regularly to stop the pasta sticking to the bottom of the pan, until the pasta has cooked through. Add extra stock, or just water, at any time if the soup becomes too thick. It should be the texture of a bolognese or a ragu – some movement, but not too thin.

Finally, stir through the soured cream, to melt it through the soup, then taste and adjust the seasoning, if needed. Ladle generously into bowls and swirl through an extra dollop of soured cream. Sprinkle over the crispy spring onions and finish with a crack of black pepper. Ponder whether you need a fork or a spoon for a while (I vote spoon).

Samphire & Brown Butter Bucatini

Samphire has a short season. In the UK, it's only at its best in the months of July and August, so each year when summer comes around, eating it feels like a special treat. It's a sea vegetable, grown most often in marshes, and as you would expect for a sea vegetable, it has a tangy, salty flavour. It deserves to be the star of the dish. Wrapped in butter, tossed with spaghetti.

~~~~~~~~~~~~~~~~~~~~

Cook the bucatini in well-salted water until al dente.

Meanwhile, melt the butter in a large frying pan over a low–medium heat. Let it bubble and crackle, swirling the pan occasionally, until the butter is covered with a layer of foam and the underneath has turned a golden brown. This will take 5–6 minutes. At this point, add the samphire and continue to cook for a further 2–3 minutes, still swirling occasionally, until the butter has darkened to a nutty brown colour. You don't want it to get too dark, so just keep an eye on it. Also, it will spit, so be careful.

Lift the bucatini from its pan and into the butter with a pair of tongs, bringing some of the pasta water along with it. Stir well to combine, adding a dash or two of pasta water to loosen the sauce, if needed. You're looking for a glossy silky sauce that easily coats the pasta. Taste and add a pinch of salt, if you think it needs it.

Swirl the pasta onto a plate and grate over a little Parmesan. Pair with a crisp glass of Burgundy chardonnay, for a simple but special dinner.

SERVES 4

350g bucatini
150g unsalted butter, cubed
90g samphire
salt
grated Parmesan, to serve

A Sabich Building Table

A sabich is a Middle Eastern sandwich. A beloved hearty street food, sabich is traditionally eaten for breakfast or lunch. It's a recipe of many choices – make all of the components or some of the components. Buy the sauces in, or make them yourself. It's up to you. Lay everything on the table and let your friends build their own sabich, however they might like it.

A note on amba: amba is a sharp, Middle Eastern condiment, made from pickled green mangoes. I'm told it's almost impossible to replicate accurately at home, so the recipe below is not traditional but is similar in flavour and spice.

MAKES ENOUGH FOR 10 SANDWICHES, FOR 4-6 PEOPLE

1 batch Hummus
1 batch Amba
1 batch Tahini Sauce
1 batch Quick Pickled Radish
1 batch Roasted Aubergine
10 Jammy Eggs
1 batch Chopped Salad
10 fluffy pitta breads (the nicest ones you can find)

Make the sabich components using the recipes below and over the next two pages. Toast the pitta breads and arrange them on the table with the rest of the components. Let your friends help themselves, stuffing all or some of the components generously into the warm toasted pitta bread. Personally, I'll have everything, all in one pitta. Why not?

HUMMUS

400g jar chickpeas, drained and rinsed
1 garlic clove, peeled
1 heaped tbsp tahini
½ tsp cumin
juice of ½ lemon
extra virgin olive oil
salt and freshly ground black pepper

Combine the chickpeas, garlic, tahini, cumin, lemon juice and a really good pinch of salt and black pepper in a food processor or high-powered blender. Blitz the mixture, adding 4–5 tbsp olive oil in a thin stream through the feed tube, until the hummus is smooth and creamy. Taste and adjust the seasoning, if needed. Refrigerate until ready to serve.

AMBA

neutral oil
1 garlic clove, sliced
½ tsp mustard seeds
½ tsp cumin seeds
pinch of cayenne pepper
½ tsp smoked paprika
¼ tsp ground turmeric
1 ripe mango, peeled, stone removed and chopped into small chunks
juice and zest of 1 lime
1 tbsp white wine vinegar
salt and freshly ground black pepper

Heat a good glug of neutral oil in a small frying pan over a low–medium heat. Once hot, add the garlic, mustard seeds, cumin seeds, cayenne pepper, smoked paprika, turmeric and a pinch of salt and fry for a minute or so, stirring constantly, until the garlic is golden and the spices are releasing their fragrance.

Remove the pan from the heat and pour its contents into a food processor or blender. Add the mango, juice and zest of your lime, white wine vinegar and a good pinch of salt and black pepper. Blitz until smooth, then taste and adjust the seasoning, if needed. Refrigerate until ready to serve.

WHIPPED TAHINI SAUCE

125g tahini
juice of ½ lemon
1 tsp olive oil
4 tbsp plain yoghurt
1 tsp runny honey, maple syrup or any other liquid sweetener
salt and freshly ground black pepper

Combine the tahini, lemon juice, olive oil, yoghurt, honey and a good pinch of salt and black pepper in a mixing bowl. Add 75ml of cold water and whisk well to combine, until creamy and lighter in colour. Taste and adjust the seasoning, if needed. Refrigerate until ready to serve.

QUICK PICKLED RADISH

100g radishes, trimmed and very finely sliced (use a mandoline, if you have one)
75ml white wine vinegar
1 tbsp caster sugar
50ml boiling water
salt

Combine the radishes, white wine vinegar, caster sugar and a pinch of salt in a bowl. Use your fingers to massage the sugar and salt into the radishes for a minute or so, until they are turning a little pink. Add 50ml of just-boiled water, then give everything a stir. Let them sit and macerate whilst you make the other components. Drain just before serving.

ROASTED AUBERGINE

4 aubergines, sliced into 2cm-thick rounds
olive oil
1 tbsp capers, finely chopped
small handful of parsley, leaves picked and roughly chopped
1 garlic clove, grated
1 tbsp white wine vinegar
salt and freshly ground black pepper

Heat the oven to 180°C fan/390°F/gas 6.

Combine the rounds of aubergine with a really good glug of olive oil and a pinch of salt and black pepper in a mixing bowl. Use your hands to give everything a mix, then divide the rounds evenly between two large baking trays. Roast for 30–40 minutes, turning them over once halfway through, until they are darkly golden and soft all the way through.

Combine the still-warm aubergine with the capers, parsley, garlic, white wine vinegar and a pinch of salt and black pepper in a mixing bowl. Stir well, then taste and adjust the seasoning if needed. Set aside until ready to serve.

JAMMY EGGS

10 eggs

Bring a large pan of water to a rolling boil. Carefully add the eggs and set the timer for 7 minutes, which will give you the perfect jammy yolks.

After 7 minutes, drain the eggs and run them under cold water, until they are cool enough to touch. Peel away their skins and chop into halves, or quarters, when ready to serve.

CHOPPED SALAD

100g baby cucumbers, finely chopped
150g good juicy tomatoes, finely chopped
½ small red onion, finely sliced
juice of ½ lemon
handful of mint, leaves picked
handful of parsley, leaves picked
extra virgin olive oil
salt and freshly ground black pepper

Combine the baby cucumbers, tomatoes, red onion, lemon juice, mint, parsley, a glug of extra virgin olive oil and a pinch of salt and black pepper in a mixing bowl. Give everything a good stir, then taste and adjust the seasoning, if needed. Refrigerate until ready to serve.

Gooseberry Cake with Honey & Thyme Cream

The sharpness of gooseberry is its charm. We had a gooseberry bush in our wild garden when I was a child and picking a gooseberry straight from the bush and popping it into my mouth was more satisfying than a sour sweet. They are made to be in puddings – their sourness calling out to be balanced with sugar and fat.

Their season is very short, so make this while you can.

CUTS INTO 8

250ml milk
2 tsp white wine vinegar
zest of 1 lemon
200g caster sugar
190g plain flour
3 tsp baking powder
200g ground almonds
pinch of salt
85g unsalted butter, melted
200g gooseberries, hard ends trimmed

CRUMBLE TOPPING
20g ground almonds
20g plain flour
20g golden caster sugar
25g unsalted butter, chilled and cubed
10g flaked almonds

HONEY & THYME CREAM
200ml whipping cream
1 tbsp runny honey
3 sprigs of thyme, leaves picked and finely chopped

Preheat the oven to 160°C fan/350°F/gas 4 and grease and/or line a high-sided cake tin. Mine is 23cm in diameter, but slightly smaller is fine.

Combine the milk and white wine vinegar in a large jug and stir well. Let it sit for 15 minutes, so it thickens and curdles slightly.

Meanwhile, make the crumble topping. Combine the ground almonds, flour and sugar in a mixing bowl. Add the butter and use the tips of your fingers to rub the butter into the flour mixture, until you have something which resembles rough breadcrumbs. Stir through the flaked almonds, then set aside.

Combine the lemon zest and sugar in a mixing bowl. Use your fingers to rub the lemon zest into the sugar (this releases the oils and increases its intensity). Next, sift the flour and baking powder into the mixture, add the ground almonds and salt and give everything a mix to combine. Stir the melted butter through the milk mixture, then slowly pour the wet ingredients into the dry ingredients, gently folding as you go, until smooth and just combined.

Pour the cake batter into the prepared tin and sprinkle with half the crumble topping. Scatter the gooseberries over the top, then the remaining crumble topping. Bake for 45–55 minutes, or until the cake is golden and a skewer inserted into the centre comes out clean. Allow to cool for 15 minutes in its tin, before turning out onto a wire rack and allowing it another 30 minutes before serving.

While the cake is cooling, make the cream. Combine the whipping cream, honey and chopped thyme in a mixing bowl and whisk into soft peaks. It's easier to use an electric whisk here, but I tend to use a regular hand whisk so I can see what the cream is doing. Cream is so easily over-whipped, so always stop sooner rather than later.

You can serve the cake slightly warm, or let it cool down completely – both are equally good. Whichever way you choose to eat it, just make sure it's with a big dollop of honey and thyme cream.

Strawberry & Black Pepper Granita, Clotted Cream

This was the last recipe I developed for the book, but very quickly it became a favourite. I love the pairing of strawberries and black pepper, whose spicy undertones push through the sweetness. These are classic flavours, but arranged in a different way. The granita is cold and refreshing; the clotted cream a pillow to the icy shards.

Heat a small frying pan over a low-medium heat. Once hot, add the peppercorns and toast for a minute or two, until they release their fragrance and begin to darken. Watch them carefully here, as they can burn quickly. Let them cool, then grind into a powder in a pestle and mortar.

Combine the ground black pepper, strawberries, caster sugar, vanilla bean paste and 175ml cold water in a blender. Blitz until completely smooth, then give it a taste and blend through a little more sugar, if you think it needs it. The granita will lose some of its sweetness when frozen, so it is better to have it on the sweeter side here.

Pour the strawberry purée into a container and freeze for an hour. A long, shallow Pyrex dish, or a large glass Tupperware does the job perfectly. After an hour, remove the dish from the freezer and use a fork to scrape and break up any of the frozen purée from around the edges, mixing it into the rest of the purée. Repeat this step every hour, scraping up the surface and breaking it into tiny shards, until the mixture is fully frozen and fluffy with ice crystals. It will take about 6 hours.

Serve between little bowls with a spoonful of clotted cream. It's gorgeous as it is, but becomes rather special with a glass of demi-sec Champagne to wash it down.

SERVES 6

15 black peppercorns
500g fresh ripe strawberries, hulled
80g caster sugar
½ tsp vanilla bean paste
clotted cream, to serve

Frozen Peach Bellinis

I've been to Venice twice; both times as a teenage backpacker. If I were to go now, I'd like to take a trip to Harry's Bar, the birthplace of the bellini – the extraordinary prices were out of my backpacker's budget back then. Created in Italy, the bellini is traditionally made with Prosecco, but I like Crémant here – the toasty, bready notes sitting perfectly with the peaches. Champagne works too.

MAKES 4

4 large ripe peaches
3–4 tbsp simple syrup
½ a 75cl bottle of Crémant

TO GARNISH
fresh peach slices (optional)
4 sprigs of thyme

To prepare your peaches for freezing, peel, remove the stones and chop into slices. Place them in a Tupperware container and freeze overnight, or until solid.

Once you're ready to make your cocktails, combine the frozen peaches and 3 tablespoons of simple syrup in a high-speed blender and blitz just a little, to break them up. Add the Crémant and blitz again, until smooth and slushy-like. Taste and add a little more simple syrup, if you think it needs it.

Pour the frozen bellinis into coupe glasses and garnish each with a peach slice, if you like, and a sprig of thyme.

SUMMER 145

AUTUMN

Autumn brings a new heaviness to the air, a crispness that makes me want to simmer and roast. I'm drawn to the earthy comfort of root vegetables – swede, potatoes and beetroots. And squash! So many beautiful winter squash. The first of the apples are falling from the trees, tart and fragrant, and the warmth of cinnamon and nutmeg creeps into my cooking. It's a time for slow cooking, for soups and stews that gently bubble on the stove. The days are shorter, the nights longer and there's a quiet pleasure in the ritual of cooking. Autumn is the season for turning inward, for filling the house with warmth and in return, the promise of something nourishing.

EARLY AUTUMN

Apple

Blackberry

Pear

Plum

Raspberry

Broccoli

Carrot

Globe artichoke

Samphire

Sweetcorn

Tomato

Beetroot

Cavolo nero

Celery

Chard

Leek

Marrow

Mushroom

Swede

Turnip

Winter squash

LATE AUTUMN

Apple
Blackberry
Pear
Plum
Celeriac
Broccoli
Carrot
Chicory
Kale

Beetroot
Cavolo nero
Celery
Chard
Leek
Marrow
Mushroom
Swede
Turnip
Winter squash

Sticky Peanut Swede

Swede, with its golden and purple tinted skin, has the kind of humble charm that gets lost amongst more glamorous vegetables. But, peel away that tough exterior and you're left with a soft, buttery sweetness that rewards you for your gentle hand and patience. Roast it, mash it or par-boil and fry it, as we are doing here. The sticky peanut sauce is moreish, but you could omit it in favour of just a good pinch of salt and black pepper to let the swede really sing, if you like. It's an easy, unexpected side dish.

Bring a large pan of salted water to the boil. Add the swede, bring the water back to a boil and cook for 6 minutes, until slightly softened. Drain and let it steam dry.

Heat a medium frying pan over a medium heat and add enough neutral oil to coat the bottom. Once hot, add the par-boiled swede and fry for 8–10 minutes, turning them every few minutes, until all sides are a rich golden brown.

Meanwhile, combine the soy sauce, runny honey, rice vinegar and peanut butter in a small bowl and mix well, until smooth.

Use a slotted spoon to remove the swede from the pan, draining off any excess oil as you do so. Drain most of the neutral oil from the pan, leaving about a tablespoon behind, then return the pan to a medium heat. Add both the swede and the sauce to the pan and let the sauce bubble and thicken and coat the swede as you stir. Cook for a further 2–3 minutes, until the sauce is sticky and reduced around the cubes of golden swede.

Spoon the swede into a serving dish and top with the roasted salted peanuts. It's perfect eaten alongside curries, on your sushi bowls or as part of a spread. I have to admit, I'll just eat it straight out of the pan.

SERVES 4, AS A SIDE

- 1 swede, peeled and chopped into 2.5cm cubes
- neutral oil
- 3 tbsp soy sauce
- 3 tbsp runny honey
- 2 tbsp rice vinegar
- 2 tbsp smooth peanut butter
- chopped roasted salted peanuts, to serve

Spicy Sweet Seeds

If you make your way through these recipes, you'll be eating a lot of squash, leaving you with plenty of seeds. I like to make this salty-sweet snack with them.

You can easily double, triple or even quadruple this recipe. I save the washed seeds in the fridge and make it all in one go. These are photographed with the Butternut Squash & Barley Bowls, Halloumi Croutons on page 160.

Preheat the oven to 140°C fan/320°F/gas 3 and line a baking tray with baking paper.

Begin by cleaning your seeds. Place them in a big bowl of water and use your hands to separate the seeds from any of the squash flesh still attached. Drain the seeds through a sieve, washing off any remaining flesh as you do, then dry them thoroughly with a tea towel.

Combine the dry, clean seeds with 2 teaspoons of the sugar, the soy sauce, hot sauce, neutral oil and a really good pinch of salt in a bowl and stir well, to coat them evenly in the seasonings. Spread them out on the lined baking tray and roast for 26–28 minutes, stirring them twice throughout, until they have hardened and are deep golden brown. Remove from the oven and stir through the remaining teaspoon of brown sugar. They will crunch up as they cool.

Let them cool completely, before storing in an airtight container, or eating them straight from the tray.

MAKES ENOUGH FOR A FEW SERVINGS

seeds from one squash or pumpkin, or 2 little ones
3 tsp light brown soft sugar
½ tsp soy sauce
1 generous tsp hot sauce
2 tsp neutral oil
salt

A Blackberry Grilled Cheese

The autumn cheese toastie of dreams. Think of the blackberries as a chutney, giving a much-needed sweetness to the salty cheese. It's what I'll eat when I am feeling a little bit hungover and want something buttery and substantial, but still fresh and tasty.

Liberally butter both sides of both slices of bread, right up to the edges. Roughly mash the blackberries on a chopping board and spread over one of the slices of bread. Layer the Brie and Cheddar on top of the blackberries, drizzle over a little honey and grind over black pepper. Place the other slice of bread on top and press it down gently.

Heat a medium frying pan (with a lid if you have one) over a low–medium heat. I always use a cast-iron pan for this. Fry the sandwich for 2–3 minutes each side, pressing it down with a spatula occasionally, until the bread is golden and the cheese is melty. Flip it over carefully! If it's browning too quickly, lower the heat slightly and put a lid on the pan. You want the bread to toast at the same speed the cheese melts.

Slice in half with a sharp knife and eat immediately, admiring the cheese pull as you do.

MAKES 1

2 slices really nice bread
salted butter, at room temperature
small handful of blackberries
40g Brie, thinly sliced
40g mature Cheddar, grated
runny honey, to drizzle
freshly ground black pepper

Warm Squash Salad & Hazelnut Salsa

SERVES 2, WITH LEFTOVERS

2 small acorn squash, skin left on, seeds removed and chopped into wedges
6 garlic cloves, peeled and bashed
4 sprigs of rosemary
olive oil
150g ball good quality mozzarella, torn into chunks
400g jar butter beans, drained and rinsed
salt and freshly ground black pepper

HAZELNUT SALSA
5 tbsp extra virgin olive oil
½ small onion, finely chopped
1 garlic clove, minced
1 red chilli, deseeded and finely chopped
30g toasted blanched hazelnuts, roughly chopped
handful of mint, leaves picked and finely chopped

Acorn squash, with its petal-like curves, is one of the lesser-used squashes. Its orange flesh roasts up into a glorious sweetness; tender and buttery. It's worth hunting it down, but you can substitute it with another squash, if that's what you have – I recommend butternut, Crown Prince or Delica.

Preheat the oven to 160°C fan/350°F/gas 4.

Combine the squash, bashed garlic and rosemary on a baking tray, drizzle with a really good glug of olive oil and sprinkle with a pinch of salt and black pepper. Use your hands to give everything a good mix and sit the garlic and rosemary within the curves of the squash. Roast for 45–50 minutes, turning them halfway through, until the squash is tender and deeply golden around the edges. You can discard the garlic and rosemary now, they've done their job.

Fifteen minutes before the squash is due out of the oven, you can make the hazelnut salsa. Heat the extra virgin olive oil in a medium frying pan over a medium heat. Once hot add the onion and fry for 6–8 minutes, stirring regularly, until lightly golden. Add the garlic, chilli and hazelnuts and fry for a further 2–3 minutes, until both the garlic and chilli have softened. Remove from the heat, then stir though the mint and a good pinch of salt. Taste and adjust the seasoning, if needed.

Arrange the roasted squash, torn mozzarella and butter beans on a serving dish. Drizzle with the hazelnut salsa, then finish with a good crack of black pepper and tuck in. It's so good.

Golden Beetroot & Fig Salad

SERVES 2

2 golden beetroots, peeled
200g chèvre blanc goat's cheese, cut into two thick rounds and rind kept on
2 tsp brown sugar
3 ripe figs, quartered
2 handfuls salad leaves (something hardy and bitter – radicchio is always nice, especially if you can get your hands on the Castelfranco variety)
small handful of toasted pecans, roughly chopped
salt and freshly ground black pepper

DRESSING
2 tbsp extra virgin olive oil
2 tbsp white wine vinegar
1 tbsp maple syrup
1 tsp wholegrain mustard

This is a sunny salad for autumn, golden like a bright, crisp day. If you can't get your hands on golden beetroots, then classic purple ones will do the job too. They have a more robust flavour, less sweet and tender, but that's okay. It will still be delicious.

First, make the dressing. Combine the extra virgin olive oil, white wine vinegar, maple syrup, wholegrain mustard and a good pinch of salt and black pepper in a shallow bowl. Taste and adjust the seasoning, if needed.

Use a mandoline to slice the beetroot as finely as you can into your dressing. If you don't have a mandoline, a speed peeler will do the job. Stir to coat all the slices of beetroot in the dressing, then let them sit and macerate for 30 minutes, giving them a mix halfway through.

Preheat the grill to medium.

When the beetroot has almost finished macerating, arrange the goat's cheese on a baking tray and sprinkle the top side of each round evenly with the brown sugar. Grill for 2–4 minutes, or until the sugar has melted and the top of the cheese is a rich golden brown.

Arrange the macerated beetroot, figs and salad leaves on a serving plate, leaving the dressing behind in its bowl. Top with the goat's cheese and a few crushed pecans, then spoon over a little extra dressing. Finish with a pinch of flaky salt and a good crack of black pepper and you're good to go.

AUTUMN 155

Squash & Sweet Chilli Salad

Underneath the Crown Prince's grey-blue skin, you'll find a luscious golden flesh. It's not an everyday squash, but when you find one (and they are getting much easier to find), pick up a few and store them somewhere dry, at room temperature. They will keep for a good few months.

Much like the butternut, the Crown Prince is an all-rounder and the flesh is dense, so it keeps its shape. It can be roasted, mashed, made into soups, stew or curries. The sweet, caramelized flesh calls out for a salty and sharp pairing, like goat's cheese. This is a simple dish. A celebration of autumn.

SERVES 2

1 large Crown Prince squash, peeled and cubed
olive oil
100g goat's cheese, cut into wedges
handful of mint leaves
small handful of toasted pine nuts
salt and freshly ground black pepper

SWEET CHILLI SAUCE
1 red chilli, very finely sliced (I don't deseed it, but you can if you like less heat)
50ml rice vinegar
2 tbsp caster sugar
1 tsp cornflour, combined with 1 tbsp water to make a slurry
½ garlic clove, grated

Preheat the oven to 200°C fan/425°F/gas 7.

Combine the squash, a really good drizzle of olive oil and a generous pinch of salt in a baking tray. Use your hands to give everything a mix, then roast for 30–40 minutes, stirring halfway through, until tender all the way through and deeply golden at the edges.

Next, make the sweet chilli sauce. Combine the sliced chilli, rice vinegar, caster sugar, cornflour slurry, grated garlic, 2 tablespoons of water and a good pinch of salt in a small saucepan. Stir well, then place over a medium heat. Bring the pan to a gentle simmer and cook, stirring constantly, for 2–3 minutes, until the sauce has reduced to a clear syrupy liquid. Remove from the heat.

Arrange the warm roasted squash and goat's cheese on a serving plate. Spoon over the warm sweet chilli sauce, then sprinkle with the mint leaves and toasted pine nuts. Finish with a good crack of black pepper and devour in one go.

Black Rice & Sweet Potato Salad

I met James towards the end of the coronavirus lockdown. Very few restaurants had reopened so, for our third date, I offered to make him dinner on my balcony. I really quite liked him, and I wanted to impress (but without seeming to try too hard, of course), so among a few other snacky bits, I settled on this. It never occurred to me at the time that this could be the first dish of many that I would share with my soulmate. But that's how life works out sometimes. Magical, isn't it?

~~~~~~~~~~~~~~~~~~~~

Preheat the oven to 200°C fan/425°F/gas 7.

Start by making the dressing. Combine the white wine vinegar, apple cider vinegar, maple syrup, extra virgin olive oil and a good pinch of salt and black pepper in a mixing bowl. Season to taste.

Add the sliced red cabbage and red onion to the dressing and stir well to combine. Let it sit and macerate at room temperature while you continue with the recipe.

Next, combine the rounds of sweet potato with a good glug of olive oil and pinch of salt and black pepper in another mixing bowl. Use your hands to give everything a mix, then arrange between two baking trays and roast for 30 minutes.

Pat the chickpeas dry with a tea towel and combine with a glug of olive oil and a pinch of salt and black pepper in a bowl. Flip the rounds of sweet potato over, then sprinkle the chickpeas on top, dividing them between the two trays. Return to the oven for a further 25–35 minutes, until the sweet potatoes have caramelized at the edges and the chickpeas are crispy.

Meanwhile, cook the black rice in salted water, according to the packet instructions.

To serve, spoon the black rice onto a large platter, or between plates. Layer the rocket, roasted sweet potato and chickpeas, coriander and macerated red cabbage and onion over the top, then finish with a few extra spoonfuls of the dressing and a crack of black pepper. Eat warm.

SERVES 4-6

- ⅛ red cabbage, very thinly sliced
- 1 red onion, very finely sliced
- 800g sweet potato, skins scrubbed and sliced into 1.5cm rounds
- olive oil
- 400g tin chickpeas, drained and rinsed
- 175g black rice, rinsed
- 2 handfuls of wild rocket
- handful of coriander leaves
- salt and freshly ground black pepper

DRESSING

- 50ml white wine vinegar
- 50ml apple cider vinegar
- 50ml maple syrup
- 50ml extra virgin olive oil

Lovely Autumn Veg & Grains with a Ginger Soy Dressing

SERVES 2

400g beetroot (roughly 3-4), scrubbed and chopped into wedges
300g butternut squash (roughly ½), peeled and chopped into chunks
300g sweet potato (1 large, or 2 medium), peeled and cubed
6 garlic cloves, peeled and bashed
olive oil
250g cooked mixed grains (you can use packet grains for ease)
juice of ½ lime
handful of mint, leaves picked
handful of coriander, leaves picked
small handful of roasted salted peanuts, roughly chopped, to serve
salt

DRESSING
2 tbsp toasted sesame oil
2 tbsp soy sauce
2 tbsp rice vinegar
1 tbsp brown sugar
2 tbsp tahini
2 garlic cloves, peeled
thumb-sized piece of ginger, peeled and roughly chopped

In the autumn months, I'll often make something like this for lunch. Fresh yet comforting, it keeps and travels well, and is easily doubled or tripled, making it perfect for meal prepping. Sometimes I add a jar or tin of butter beans or cooked cubes of firm tofu if I have them to hand.

You'll probably end up with some leftover butternut squash, which is never a bad thing in my view. You can use it in my Butternut Squash & Black Rice Soup Bowls on page 168, or the Squash & Sweet Chilli Salad on page 156.

Preheat the oven to 180°C fan/390°F/gas 6.

Combine the beetroot, butternut squash, sweet potato and bashed garlic on a large baking tray. Drizzle with a really good glug of olive oil and a pinch of salt. Use your hands to give everything a good mix, nestling the garlic between the vegetables. Roast for 40-50 minutes, giving everything a mix halfway through, until the veg is golden and tender all the way through. You can discard the garlic now - it's done its job.

Meanwhile, make the dressing. Combine the toasted sesame oil, soy sauce, rice vinegar, brown sugar, tahini, garlic and ginger in a small food processor. Blitz until smooth and combined, then taste and add a pinch of salt, if you think it needs it. If you don't have a small food processor, you could use a hand blender, or grate the ginger and garlic and whisk all the ingredients together. Drizzle a few spoonfuls over the tray of roasted veg and give them a good mix, to coat.

Warm through the grains (if you're using a packet, you'll do this in the microwave) and combine with the lime juice and most of the mint and coriander in a mixing bowl.

Divide the grains between shallow bowls and top with the roasted vegetables. Drizzle each one with a little extra dressing and finish with a good sprinkling of roasted salted peanuts and the remaining mint and coriander.

Butternut Squash & Barley Bowls, Halloumi Croutons

There is comfort in the chewy bite of pearl barley. Reassuringly substantial. It lends itself well to soups and stews, absorbing and savouring the flavours of the stock. This is a hob-only recipe, the sugars in the butternut squash caramelizing in the pan. Try not to skimp on this step. Let the chunks of squash fry to a rich golden brown – it will make all the difference.

You can make this with or without the halloumi croutons, but I think they are a nice salty and crunchy addition. In this photo I've also topped with the Spicy Sweet Seeds (see page 151).

Combine the porcini mushrooms and 200ml of just-boiled water in a jug. Let them sit and infuse while you continue with the recipe.

Next, heat a large heavy-bottomed pan over a medium heat and add enough olive oil to coat the bottom. Once hot, fry the chunks of butternut squash and a pinch of salt for 15–18 minutes, turning them every few minutes, until they are golden on all sides. Use a slotted spoon to remove them from the pan and set them aside for later.

In the same pan, still set over a medium heat, fry the onion and a pinch of salt for 6–8 minutes, stirring regularly, until soft and translucent. You can add a dash more olive oil if you need to. Add the garlic and fry for a minute or so, just to soften.

Stir the pearl barley through the pan, to coat it in the oil. Add the porcini mushrooms and their stock, 1.5 litres of just-boiled water, the thyme and a really good pinch of salt and black pepper, then bring the pan to a boil. Reduce the heat to low and simmer gently for 20–25 minutes, stirring occasionally, until the pearl barley is al dente.

Stir the butternut squash through the pan and continue to cook for a further 30–35 minutes, or until it is gorgeous and buttery and tender and the pearl barley has cooked through. Add extra water at any point if the pan becomes too dry. It should be the texture of a thick stew – some movement, but not too thin. Stir through the white wine vinegar, then taste and adjust the seasoning, if needed.

When you are a few minutes from serving, heat a glug of olive oil in a medium frying pan over a medium heat. Once hot, fry the halloumi for 2–3 minutes each side, until lightly golden.

Fish out the thyme, then ladle the stew into bowls. Top with a good drizzle of extra virgin olive oil, halloumi croutons and a good crack of black pepper. Cosy up and eat with a spoon.

SERVES 4

- 30g dried porcini mushrooms
- 200ml boiling water
- olive oil
- 1 medium butternut squash, peeled, deseeded and chopped into chunky cubes
- 1 large onion, finely chopped
- 4 garlic cloves, minced
- 300g pearl barley
- 1.5 litres boiling water
- 6 sprigs of thyme
- 1 tbsp white wine vinegar
- 250g halloumi, chopped into small cubes
- salt and freshly ground black pepper
- extra virgin olive oil, to serve

SQUASH

SQUASH 101
There are two categories of squash: summer squash and winter squash. Summer squash have tender, edible skins, edible flowers and a mild creamy flesh; courgettes, Patty Pan, Crookneck. Winter squash are at their best between the start of autumn and the start of winter and are our focus here. They have hard skins, dense sweet flesh and large mature seeds. To cook only with butternut squash is a shame. It's a privilege to experiment – mix it up. Cook with the prettiest or most eccentric squash you can find, using this guide to help you.

Just a quick note to save confusion – what we know as 'pumpkins' are all varieties of winter squash. There is no botanical distinction for which winter squash are called pumpkins, instead we differentiate only by appearance – harder skinned, round, squat. The classic 'pumpkin' shape. Below I call what you may know as a 'pumpkin' by the botanical name of 'squash'.

ACORN
Small and round with a pointed bottom, Acorn squash has a ribbed dark green or yellow skin and a soft yellow-orange flesh which roasts up until sweet and slightly nutty. It is ideal for roasting, stuffing with grains and vegetables or using in soups. Roasted in halves, it pairs nicely with a sweet cinnamon butter as a snack or dessert.

BUTTERCUP
Also known as Bonbon squash, Buttercup squash is small to medium in size with deep, dark green skin and a distinctive round indentation on top. Its earthy, dense, dry flesh roasts up to a rich honey-like sweetness. Ideal for pumpkin pie and other desserts, roasting, mashing or using in soups.

BUTTERNUT
The ever popular butternut squash has the highest proportion of flesh to cavity. It has a long neck, with smooth, thin tan skin and creamy sweet orange flesh. It is ideal for roasting, mashing, using in soups, purées and desserts.

CARNIVAL
The Carnival squash is a hybrid of the acorn and sweet dumpling squash. It is small and round with vibrant bright orange, green and cream-yellow striped and speckled skin and a mild, sweet slightly nutty flesh. It is ideal for roasting or stuffing with grains and vegetables.

CROWN PRINCE
The medium–large Crown Prince has a distinctive blue-grey ridged skin and a rich, deep orange flesh. Its dense flesh keeps its shape when cooked and roasts up until sweet, smooth and slightly nutty. It is ideal for roasting, mashing, using in curries, stews and soups and for sweet or savoury pies.

DELICATA
A cylindrical squash, Delicata has yellow–cream thin skin and vertical green stripes. It has a mild, sweet, creamy flesh with a flavour reminiscent of sweetcorn. It's ideal for baking whole (no need to peel), chopping and roasting or stuffing with vegetables and grains.

HUBBARD
The Hubbard squash is large and round with pointed ends. It has blue, golden or green rough bumpy skin and very sweet, dry starchy flesh. Ideal for pumpkin pie, mashing or using in soups and casseroles.

KABOCHA
Also known as Japanese or Delica pumpkin, Kabocha is round and squat, with dark green or orange skin and dense, rich, bright orange flesh. Often compared to a cross between pumpkin and sweet potato, they are ideal roasted in wedges, steamed, in curries and stews, mashed and used in soups or purées.

MASHED POTATO

The Mashed Potato squash is small to medium in size with pale yellow skin and a ribbed, egg-like shape. Its flesh is mildly sweet with a creamy, starchy texture which roasts up to a buttery smoothness. Ideal for roasting and mashing to use as an alternative to mashed potato, puréeing and blending into soups.

RED KURI

Red Kuri squash is small and teardrop-shaped with bright red-orange skin and a sweet, smooth buttery flesh. Ideal for roasting, eating warm in salads and using in soups, purées and desserts.

SPAGHETTI

This squash is large and oblong with yellow skin and mild stringy flesh that shreds into spaghetti-like strands. It can be roasted or sautéed and treated similar to spaghetti – topped with or stirred through sauce.

SWEET DUMPLING

The Sweet Dumpling squash is small and round with pale cream skin, distinctive dark green stripes and very sweet, smooth yellow-orange flesh. Ideal for roasting, stuffing with grains and vegetables, or eating in warm salads.

Autumn Pasta with Chickpeas

This is inspired by the Italian dish pasta e ceci, which translates to 'pasta with chickpeas'. As Rachel Roddy puts it in her book *An A–Z of Pasta*, 'there are as many versions as cooks,' and I like to make this version in the autumn, when the air has a slight chill. It will warm the soul.

We are using Kabocha squash here for its dense sweet flesh. But you can substitute it with any squash suited to roasting: butternut, Crown Prince or Bonbon.

Preheat the oven to 180°C fan/390°F/gas 6.

Combine the squash with a good glug of olive oil and a pinch of salt and black pepper on a baking tray. Roast for around 35–40 minutes, mixing halfway through, until tender in the middle and golden on the edges. Allow to cool enough to touch, then remove the skin of half the squash and roughly mash its flesh, keeping the other half of the chunks whole. Set both aside.

Heat a good glug of olive oil in a large saucepan set over a medium heat. Once hot, add the onion and a pinch of salt and fry, stirring frequently, for 6–8 minutes, until soft and translucent. Add the garlic and tomato purée and fry for a further minute or so, just to soften.

Stir through the ditaloni pasta and pour in the stock. Bring everything to a boil, then reduce the heat to simmer and cook for 5–6 minutes (stirring regularly to stop the pasta sticking to the bottom of the pan) until the pasta is al dente.

Add the mashed squash, chickpeas and cavolo nero and bring the pan back to a simmer. Cook for a further 3–4 minutes, to wilt the cavolo nero and warm through the chickpeas, adding extra stock (or just boiling water) if the pan becomes too dry. It's a very thick soup, but you still want some movement in there. Remove from the heat and taste and adjust the seasoning, if needed.

Meanwhile, heat a really good glug of olive oil in a small frying pan over a medium–high heat. Once hot, add the sage leaves and fry for 20–30 seconds, until crisp. Use a slotted spoon to remove them from the oil and onto a sheet of kitchen towel, to soak up any excess grease.

Ladle the soup between bowls and top with the cubes of roasted squash, a few crispy sage leaves, a nice grating of Parmesan and a crack of black pepper. Cosy up and dig in.

SERVES 4

- 1 large Kabocha squash, deseeded and diced into chunks (skin left on)
- olive oil
- 1 onion, finely chopped
- 3 garlic cloves, minced
- 1 tbsp tomato purée
- 150g ditaloni (or any other small pasta shape)
- 1 litre vegetable stock
- 700g jar chickpeas, drained and rinsed (largest chickpeas are best here)
- 2 handfuls of cavolo nero, hard stems removed, roughly chopped
- 16 sage leaves
- salt and freshly ground black pepper
- grated Parmesan, to serve

Butternut Squash & Black Rice Soup Bowls

I went to a very small school for my final years of secondary school. There wasn't a canteen so instead, a series of microwaves lined the countertops of the shared kitchen. Some of us brought in leftovers from the night before, some of us ready meals, but most of us, soup. It was the type of soup you buy in the plastic tub; too much for one person, too little for two. There was nothing necessarily wrong with it, but I avoided soup for years after that. The smell of it taking me back to the cramped kitchen and teenagers fighting to be next in line to warm their food.

It wasn't until I started cooking professionally that I saw soup not only as a convenience, but as a comfort. Recipe developer Fran Allen introduced me to the concept of a soup bowl (soup with lots of added extras) and she inspired this dish.

Sometimes I'll just make this soup on its own, without the rice, adding a tin of drained and rinsed cannellini beans along with 150ml of extra stock and blending as usual. The beans aren't essential, but will make the soup a more substantial stand-alone meal. It freezes well like this too.

SERVES 3–4

800g butternut squash, peeled and chopped into chunks
neutral oil
200g black rice, rinsed
1 onion, finely chopped
3 garlic cloves, minced
thumb-sized piece of ginger, finely sliced
1 red chilli, deseeded and finely sliced
2 tbsp miso paste
600–700ml vegetable stock
400g tin coconut milk
salt and freshly ground black pepper

TO SERVE
cream
chilli crisp oil
sesame seeds
coriander leaves

Preheat the oven to 180°C fan/390°F/gas 6.

Combine the butternut squash, a good drizzle of oil and a pinch of salt and black pepper on a baking tray. Use your hands to give everything a mix, then roast for 35–40 minutes, mixing halfway through, until the squash is soft and slightly golden.

Cook the black rice in salted water, according to the packet instructions.

Meanwhile, heat a large saucepan over a medium heat and add a good glug of oil. Once hot, add the onion and a pinch of salt and fry for 6–8 minutes, until soft and translucent. Add the garlic, ginger and red chilli and fry for a further 2–3 minutes, just to soften slightly.

Next, add the miso paste, vegetable stock (start with 600ml and you can always add more when blending the soup, if you find it's too thick), coconut milk, most of the roasted butternut squash and a good pinch of salt to the pan. Stir well to combine, then bring everything to a gentle simmer and cook for 6–8 minutes, to slightly reduce. Use a hand blender to blitz it into a silky smooth soup, adding a little extra stock, if it's too thick for you (you can also do this in a stand blender, just let it cool down slightly first). Taste and adjust the seasoning, if needed.

Scoop a few spoonfuls of black rice into each of your bowls and ladle the soup over the top. Now for the toppings: a swirl of cream, the remaining roasted butternut squash, a spoonful of chilli crisp, a sprinkling of sesame seeds, a few coriander leaves and a good crack of black pepper.

Roasted Beetroot & Wasabi Soup

I love dinners that are nice and straightforward, but with a special twist. This book is full of them. You think you are sipping on a crimson velvety soup, but then it lights a little unexpected fire on your tongue. Surprising and appreciated. The wasabi could be swapped out for a more classic beetroot pairing of horseradish, if that's what you have, but either way, the amount relies on your tastebuds.

I like this with two teaspoons of wasabi added before boiling, to soften its flavour into an undertone, then half a teaspoon added while blending the soup to bring its punchy flavour forward. You may prefer it simply with one teaspoon added to the soup when boiling. Play around; see what you like.

Preheat the oven to 180°C fan/390°F/gas 6.

Scrub the beetroots under running water until they are clean and bright purple. Fold them into a tight parcel of baking parchment or tin foil (this helps them to steam as they bake), then place them on a baking tray and bake for 1 hour 15 minutes–1 hour 30 minutes, or until the beetroot can be pierced through easily with a knife. Once they are cool enough to touch, chop them into rough chunks.

Warm a good glug of olive oil in a large saucepan over a medium heat. Once hot, add the onion and a pinch of salt and fry for 6–8 minutes, stirring regularly, until soft and translucent.

Add the baked beetroot, cannellini beans, vegetable stock and wasabi (start with less – you can always add more later) to the saucepan. Bring everything to a gentle simmer and cook for 6–8 minutes, stirring constantly, to slightly reduce the stock and soften the beans. Remove from the heat and use a hand blender to blitz it into a silky smooth soup. If you would prefer it thinner, you can either make up a little extra stock to blend through, or just use water (you can also do this in a stand blender, just let it cool down slightly first). Taste and adjust the seasoning and the wasabi, blending through more, if needed.

Ladle the soup into bowls. It needs nothing more than a swirl of cream, a glug of your best extra virgin olive oil and a grind of black pepper. I don't think it even needs bread, but obviously, you do as you wish.

SERVES 4

500g raw beetroot (about 4–5), topped and tailed
olive oil
1 onion, finely chopped
400g tin cannellini beans, drained and rinsed
700ml vegetable stock
1–2 tsp wasabi paste
salt and freshly ground black pepper

TO SERVE
double cream
extra virgin olive oil

Griddled Hispi Cabbage & Charred Jalapeño Sauce

Hispi cabbage has quite a long season. I've put it in the autumn section of this book as it seems to be a vegetable I reach for more at this time of year. Maybe it's the heartier nature of the cabbage. I eat this on its own, as I think it works wonderfully as a stand-alone dish, but it's also good as a side dish, or as part of a BBQ spread in the summer. In fact, if you have the BBQ on, you could griddle the hispi cabbage on there and char the jalapeños in the coals.

Preheat the oven to 180°C fan/390°F/gas 6.

Slice off the top of the garlic bulb, to reveal the top of the cloves. Drizzle with a little olive oil and a sprinkle of salt, then wrap tightly in foil and place in a small baking dish. Roast for 35–40 minutes, or until the garlic is tender enough to squeeze.

Meanwhile, heat a glug of olive oil in a griddle pan over a medium–high heat. Once hot, griddle the hispi cabbage for 3–4 minutes each side, until darkly golden and charred with griddle marks. You could also do this in a regular frying pan – you just won't get the char marks. Transfer to a baking tray, sprinkle with a good pinch of salt, and roast alongside the garlic for 20–25 minutes, or until tender all the way through.

While the cabbage is roasting, use tongs to burn your jalapeños over the flame of a gas stove, until the skin has blackened evenly all over. If you don't have a gas stove, you can roast them alongside the garlic, until the skin is dark and charred. Allow to cool slightly, then chop off the stalks and use your fingers to scrape off the charred skin. I find it the least messy way to do this is under a running tap, so give that a go.

Combine the tahini, coriander, cumin, lemon juice and a really good pinch of salt and black pepper in a food processor. Squeeze in the flesh of the roasted garlic and add the charred jalapeños. Depending on how spicy you'd like the sauce, you can add all the jalapeños with their seeds, one or two with their seeds, or remove the seeds from all three. Blitz the mixture, adding 1 tablespoon of olive oil and 3–4 tablespoons of water in a thin stream through the tube at the top, until the sauce is smooth and creamy. It should be pourable, but not too thin. Taste and adjust the seasoning, if needed.

Arrange the roasted cabbage on a serving plate and drizzle generously with the sauce. Finish with a sprinkling of toasted sesame seeds and breadcrumbs, for a nice crunch.

SERVES 2, AS A MAIN

1 garlic bulb
extra virgin olive oil
2 hispi cabbage, quartered
3 jalapeños (or green chillies if you can't find them)
4 tbsp tahini
25g fresh coriander, hard stalks removed
½ tsp ground cumin
juice of 1 lemon
salt and freshly ground black pepper

TO SERVE
toasted sesame seeds
toasted breadcrumbs

Crimson Beetroot Dhal

Beetroot is always a welcome addition to the warm gold, rich orange and earthy green colour palette we see on our autumn plates. There are many colourful varieties, but here, only the deep, dark purple-red ones will do. Watch as you stir the silky blended beetroot through: a simple dhal is transformed into an earthy vibrant crimson. It's a beautiful thing.

SERVES 2, WITH LEFTOVERS

- 500g raw beetroot (about 4–5), peeled and chopped into wedges
- neutral oil
- 900ml vegetable stock
- 1 red onion, finely chopped
- 2 garlic cloves, minced
- thumb-sized piece of ginger, grated (I don't bother peeling it)
- 125g dried red lentils, rinsed
- 100g creamed coconut, roughly chopped
- 1 tsp sugar
- juice of ½ lemon
- salt and freshly ground black pepper

SPICE MIX
- 2 tsp garam masala
- ½ tsp chilli flakes
- ½ tsp ground coriander
- 1 tsp ground cumin
- 1 tsp ground cinnamon

TO SERVE
- plain yoghurt
- 1 tbsp chopped spring onions
- toasted cashew nuts
- handful of coriander leaves
- warm parathas

Preheat the oven to 180°C fan /390°F/gas mark 6.

Combine the beetroot with a good glug of neutral oil and a generous pinch of salt and black pepper on a baking tray. Roast for 40–45 minutes, stirring once halfway, until tender all the way through. Blitz half the roasted beetroot with 100ml of the vegetable stock in a high-powered blender until smooth and velvety, keeping the other half as it is. Set both aside for later.

Stir together the spices in a small bowl to make the spice mix.

Heat a good glug of neutral oil in a large, high-sided frying pan set over a medium heat. Once hot, add the red onion and a pinch of salt and fry for 6–8 minutes, until soft and translucent. Add the garlic, ginger and spice mix, stir well and fry for a further minute or so, until the spices release their fragrance.

Add the red lentils, creamed coconut, remaining vegetable stock, sugar and a good pinch of salt to the pan. Stir well and bring to a boil. Lower the heat to a simmer and cook for 20–25 minutes, stirring occasionally, until the lentils are soft and the dhal is creamy. If your pan becomes too dry at any point, you can add a little more liquid – either make up more vegetable stock, or just use boiling water. Once the lentils are tender, stir through the beetroot stock and lemon juice and watch the dhal slowly turn crimson as you stir. Taste and adjust the seasoning, if needed.

Ladle the dhal between bowls and top with a generous dollop of yoghurt, the remaining roasted beetroot, a few sliced spring onions, toasted cashew nuts, coriander and a good crack of black pepper. Eat with warm flaky parathas. Any leftovers will keep for a few days in the fridge.

A Deep, Dark Cavolo Nero Curry

Cavolo nero, with its dark blistered leaves, is in season from late summer until the end of autumn. I've always felt like it should be a winter vegetable; the not-quite-black leaves mirroring the shorter days in the UK. But I'm happy to have it earlier in the year. When summer produce leaves us, we have dishes like this to look forward to.

This curry works perfectly well with paneer or tofu. I use both, or sometimes a mixture of the two. I've based this on saag paneer, but it's smoother, deeper and earthier.

Eat it with naan, parathas, rice or on its own. It works gorgeously as part of a larger selection of curries, too, for very lucky friends. (See photo overleaf.)

~~~~~~~~~~~~~~~~~~~~~

Start by making the cavolo nero purée. Bring a large saucepan of salted water to a rolling boil and fill a large bowl with iced water. Add half of the cavolo nero to the boiling water and blanch for 1 minute, until just wilted. Use a slotted spoon to quickly remove it and plunge it into the iced water. Repeat with the other half of the cavolo nero (you can just plunge it on top of the other cavolo nero in the bowl of iced water). Once the cavolo nero has cooled, drain and shake out as much water as you can.

Combine the blanched cavolo nero with the green chilli, garlic, ginger, 400ml of cold water and a good pinch of salt in a high-powered blender. Blend into a smooth, velvety paste and set aside.

Next, if you are using tofu, dry the cubes with a tea towel to remove any excess liquid. If you are using paneer, you won't need to bother. Combine the cubed tofu or paneer with the garam masala, ground cumin, cornflour and a good pinch of salt in a mixing bowl and use your hands to give everything a good mix. Heat your largest frying pan over a medium heat and add enough neutral oil to coat the bottom. Once hot, add the tofu or paneer and fry for 6–8 minutes, turning it every few minutes, until crisp and golden on all sides. Use a slotted spoon to remove it from the oil and onto a few sheets of kitchen towel to soak up any excess grease.

SERVES 4

neutral oil
1 onion, finely chopped
4 garlic cloves, minced
1 tsp cumin seeds
½ tsp ground turmeric
½ tsp chilli powder
¼ tsp asafoetida
100ml passata
½ tsp garam masala
juice of ½ lemon
salt and freshly ground black pepper

CAVOLO NERO PURÉE

250g cavolo nero, weighed after hard stems removed, roughly chopped
1 green chilli, deseeded and sliced, plus extra to serve
2 garlic cloves, peeled
thumb-sized piece of ginger, sliced (I don't bother peeling it), plus extra to serve

PANEER/TOFU

500g paneer or tofu, cubed
1 tsp garam masala
2 tsp ground cumin
2 tbsp cornflour

TO SERVE

cream
naan bread

Keep the same pan with the same oil over a medium heat (don't worry about any remaining spices or cornflour in the bottom). Add the onion and fry for 4–5 minutes, stirring regularly as it sizzles in the oil, until lightly golden. Add the garlic, cumin seeds, turmeric, chilli powder, asafoetida and a pinch of salt and fry for a further minute or so, until the spices release their fragrance.

Pour the passata into the pan, and let it bubble and reduce for a minute. Stir through the cavolo nero purée and bring to a gentle simmer. Lower the heat slightly and cook, stirring regularly, for 4–5 minutes, until the sauce is glossy and has slightly reduced. Stir through the garam masala, lemon juice and paneer or tofu then remove from the heat. Season to taste with salt and black pepper.

Finish with a swirl of cream, a good crack of black pepper and some sliced ginger and chilli, if you like your spice. Serve with lots of fluffy naan bread to scoop and dip.

Colcannon Patties, Curry Mayo

Every family in Ireland will have their own version of colcannon. Mashed potato with added cabbage, onions, chives, kale, laverbread, leeks; I've tasted many. I keep mine simple – Savoy cabbage, uber creamy potatoes and loads of cream and butter. I'm making it into patties, as I can't think of a more delicious lunch, but you could stop at the mash stage for a rather wonderful side dish. Just omit the flour.

Colcannon is traditionally made by boiling the potatoes in their skins and peeling them after boiling. It's made this way to reduce the amount of water that penetrates the potatoes, creating a fluffier mash. Most often I'll cook it this way, but I have found that steam-drying the potatoes in the pan does an equally good job, with a bit less faff.

The curry mayo I think of as essential, but if that isn't quite your thing, a spoonful of mango chutney or piccalilli would go down a treat, too. (See photo on previous page.)

SERVES 4

1kg floury potatoes (I use Maris Pipers), peeled and cubed
75ml double cream
25g unsalted butter
½ Savoy cabbage, shredded
100g plain flour
olive oil
salt and freshly ground black pepper
fried eggs, to serve (if you like)

CURRY MAYO
6 tbsp good quality mayonnaise
1 tbsp mild curry powder
1 tbsp mango chutney
1 tsp rice vinegar

Start by making the mash for the patties. Bring a large pan of salted water to the boil and add the potatoes. Boil for 12–15 minutes, until the potatoes are soft enough to be easily halved with a fork. Drain, then return them to the pan and let them steam dry. Add the double cream and a pinch of salt and black pepper and mash until smooth and creamy (I use a potato ricer here, which makes a smoother mash. Not essential, but nice to have). Taste and adjust the seasoning, if needed.

Meanwhile, melt the butter in your best large frying pan over a medium heat; one that heats evenly and creates a good sear. I'll use a cast iron or stainless steel one here. Add the cabbage and a pinch of salt and fry for 5–6 minutes, stirring frequently, until the cabbage has softened and slightly wilted.

Combine the cabbage, mashed potato and 50g of the flour in a mixing bowl. Mix well, then taste and adjust the seasoning, if needed. The mixture will be thick. Allow to cool.

Meanwhile, make the curry mayo. Combine the mayo, curry powder, mango chutney, rice vinegar and a good grind of black pepper in a small bowl. Taste and add a pinch of salt, if you think it needs it.

Once the colcannon is cool enough to touch, shape it into 8 even flat patties with your hands. Combine the remaining flour with a pinch of salt and black pepper on a plate. Turn each patty over in the flour, to generously coat the top and bottom.

Wipe out your frying pan, return to a medium heat and add enough olive oil to coat the bottom. Once hot, fry the patties in two batches for 3–4 minutes undisturbed on each side, until they are crisp and deeply golden. Try not to move them too much; let them do their thing. Remove them from the oil and onto a few sheets of kitchen towel, to soak up any excess grease.

Arrange two colcannon patties on each plate, with a generous spoonful of the curry mayo on the side. Add a fried egg, if you like.

Miso Red Cabbage, Mash & Crispy Beans

It is surprisingly hard to use up a whole red cabbage. Shredding just a quarter will produce a mountain of cabbage on your chopping board; more than enough for most recipes. I no longer see this as a problem, however, only an excuse to make one of my most favourite meals; a dish to soothe and comfort.

The recipe calls for a whole red cabbage. But if you are only left with ¾ of a red cabbage, you can make the recipe work the same. For half a red cabbage, halve the recipe.

Preheat the oven to 190°C fan/410°F/gas 7.

Start by making the crispy beans. Pat the cannellini beans dry with a tea towel, then combine with the sesame oil, soy sauce, garlic and a good pinch of salt in a bowl. Pour out into one even layer on a baking tray and bake for 25–30 minutes, mixing halfway through, until golden and crispy.

To make the mash, bring a large saucepan of salted water to the boil and add the potatoes. Boil for 12–15 minutes, until the potatoes are soft enough to be easily halved with a fork. Drain, then return them to the pan and let them steam dry. Add a good glug of milk and a pinch of salt and mash until smooth and creamy (I use a potato ricer here, which makes a smoother mash. Not essential, but nice to have). Taste and adjust the seasoning, if needed.

Meanwhile, cut the red cabbage into 8 wedges, leaving the core attached. Heat a good glug of neutral oil in two large frying pans set over medium–high heat. Divide the cabbage wedges between the pans and sprinkle with a pinch of salt. Fry for 4–5 minutes on each cut side, until turning a deep brown at the edges. Pour 50ml of the stock into each pan and let it simmer and bubble for minute or so, until almost evaporated.

In a small bowl, combine the butter, miso paste and garlic. Dot the mixture evenly between the pans, then cook for a further 4–5 minutes, turning the red cabbage wedges regularly, until they are tender all the way through and the sauce is caramelized and sticky.

Divide the mash between shallow bowls and arrange the red cabbage on top. Return both frying pans to a high heat and add 50ml of water to each. Use a spatula to scrape any sticky, crispy bits off the bottom of the pan and let the sauce simmer and thicken for a minute or so. Spoon generously over the red cabbage and finish with a handful of crispy beans.

SERVES 4

- 650g floury potatoes, peeled and cubed
- milk
- neutral oil
- 1 small red cabbage
- 100ml vegetable stock
- 100g salted butter, softened at room temperature
- 3½ tbsp miso paste (I use a brown rice one, but any will do)
- 3 garlic cloves, grated
- salt

CRISPY BEANS

- 400g tin cannellini beans, drained and rinsed
- 2 tbsp toasted sesame oil
- 1 tsp soy sauce
- 1 garlic clove, grated

Baked Chard Conchiglioni

This is a dish to make unhurriedly on a Sunday afternoon; for snuggling up on the sofa with when the evening is in full swing. I use chard here, a favourite autumnal green. The hardy stalks give it more structure than spinach, which I find necessary for pairing with the gentle, soft ricotta.

~~~~~~~~~~~~~~~~~~~~

Start by making the tomato sauce. Combine the tomatoes, butter, onion, garlic, sugar, bay leaves, thyme and a good pinch of salt in a large pan set over a medium heat. Bring to a gentle simmer, then reduce the heat to low and cook for 45 minutes, stirring occasionally, until the sauce has reduced. Remove from the heat, and fish out the bay leaves and thyme. Use a hand blender to blend it into a smooth silky sauce (you can also do this in a stand blender, just let it cool down slightly first). Taste and adjust the seasoning, if needed.

Preheat the oven to 180°C fan/390°F/gas 6.

Tear the leaves of the Swiss chard from their stems. Finely chop the stems and the leaves, keeping them separate. Heat your largest frying pan over a medium heat and add a good glug of olive oil. Once hot, fry the stems of the Swiss chard, garlic and a pinch of salt for 3–4 minutes, to soften slightly. Add the chard leaves and stir for a further few minutes, until wilted.

Combine the softened Swiss chard and garlic, ricotta cheese, mascarpone, Parmesan, basil, lemon juice, nutmeg and a few really good cracks of black pepper in a mixing bowl. Give everything a good stir, then taste and adjust the seasoning, if needed.

Pour the tomato sauce into a large baking dish. Mine is 28cm square, but slightly larger will work too. Gently spoon the filling into the pasta shells, filling them right up to the top, then push the shells side-by-side into the sauce, with their filling facing up. The sauce will come up and around the sides of the shells as you continue to fill the dish. Sprinkle over the mozzarella, then cover the dish tightly with foil and bake for 1 hour. Remove the foil and bake for a further 15–20 minutes, or until the pasta has cooked through and the top is golden and bubbling.

Let the dish sit for 10 minutes before spooning into bowls. Eat it on your lap, watching a film. If you have a fire, put that on too. There is nothing quite like it.

SERVES 6

- 300g Swiss chard
- olive oil
- 2 garlic cloves, thinly sliced
- 250g ricotta cheese
- 250g mascarpone
- 75g Parmesan, finely grated
- large handful of basil, leaves picked and finely chopped
- juice of ½ lemon
- ¼ tsp freshly grated nutmeg
- 200g conchiglioni (giant pasta shells)
- 150g ball mozzarella, drained and grated
- salt and freshly ground black pepper

TOMATO SAUCE

- 4 x 400g tins whole plum tomatoes
- 100g unsalted butter
- 1 large onion, peeled and quartered
- 6 garlic cloves, peeled but left whole
- 1 tsp sugar
- 2 bay leaves
- 4 sprigs of thyme

Sweet Potato Gratin Pie

There is a very special lady in my life called Carolyn who is the best cook I know. I have had many roast dinners cooked by her, although not for many years now. Always on the table was a dish of cubed sweet potato baked in cream, cheese and more rosemary than you would think appropriate. I believe it was an invention of her own – my favourite thing she would cook. Everything was as indulgent as possible: the more butter, the better. A philosophy I live by now.

The filling of this pie is inspired by her dish. It was always the best part of her roast dinners for me, so now it can be the principal of the plate. I love it as an exquisite roast dinner main, the leftovers reheated the next day and served with a fresh, zesty salad. Maybe my Zesty Kale Salad from page 222, made with autumnal cavolo nero instead. (See photos overleaf.)

SERVES 6

1kg sweet potatoes (about 3 large or 5 medium), peeled and chopped into 2cm cubes
olive oil
400ml double cream
2 egg yolks
6 garlic cloves, minced
100g Gruyére, grated
100g extra mature Cheddar, grated
50g Parmesan, finely grated
270g packet of filo pastry
100g unsalted butter, melted
5 sprigs of rosemary, leaves picked
salt and freshly ground black pepper

Preheat the oven to 170°C fan/375°F/gas 5.

Combine the cubed sweet potato, a good glug of olive oil and a pinch of salt and black pepper on a large baking tray, or between two smaller ones. Use your hands to give everything a thorough mix, then roast for 25 minutes, stirring once halfway through, until mostly tender. Let it cool while you continue with the recipe.

Next, combine the cream, egg yolks, garlic and a good pinch of salt and black pepper in a large jug and whisk well. Combine the Gruyére, Cheddar and Parmesan in a bowl.

To make the filo pie case, unwrap the filo pastry and place a slightly damp tea towel on top of it to keep it fresh as you work. Place a sheet of filo in front of you, its long side parallel to the edge of your work surface. They are usually 45cm/46cm on their long side, but if yours are a lot shorter than this, you'll need to stick two together, to make them a similar length to mine. Gently spread the filo sheet all over with melted butter, then place another sheet on top of the first, but this time with its short side parallel to your work surface, to create a cross. Spread it with butter, then place another sheet on top, this time at a 45-degree angle to the previous sheet, then another at the opposite 45-degree angle. The idea is that you are creating a pointy circle of pastry. Continue with the rest of the filo pastry, spreading each sheet with butter and layering over the next sheet at an angle, until you have an even circle of filo pastry.

Transfer the circle of filo pastry to a high-sided springform cake tin and press gently into the bottom and sides of the pan, scrunching the filo together at the sides, to create a ruffled effect. My tin is 23cm, but you'll be fine with one a centimetre smaller or larger too.

Scatter a third of the sweet potato in the bottom of the filo case. Pour over a third of the cream mixture, a third of the cheese mixture, a third of the rosemary and a pinch of salt and black pepper. Repeat this with the remaining mixture, layering the ingredients a third at a time, until you finish with the cheese, rosemary, salt and black pepper on top. Bake for 45–50 minutes, or until the filling has set and the cheese is deeply golden on top. If you find the filo pastry is darkening too quickly, you can cover the edges of the tin with foil for the last 20 minutes or so of the cooking time.

Let the pie cool for 20 minutes, to help the filling set a little, then remove from the tin. Chop it into thick slices and eat just as it is, or if you're feeling indulgent, with your roast dinner.

Wild Mushroom Hotpot

I was lucky to grow up on some home-cooked food, but mostly, dinner times were formed of ready meals. If my dad was doing the shopping, it would be the British classics. Shepherd's pie, cottage pie, casserole, Lancashire hotpot. I still make my versions of all of them to this day.

This is how I make my Lancashire hotpot. With creamy wild mushrooms and a crisp potato top. I have served it with a fresh green salad in the past, but I hear this is sacrilege in Lancashire. Some buttery steamed cavolo nero might be more appropriate.

I don't bother peeling the potatoes here – I like how the skin gets extra crisp in the oven – but that is up to the cook. Usually, I'll make this with a packet of cooked lentils, but if you want to cook your own, use 100g of dried Puy lentils, cooked to the packet instructions. (See photos overleaf.)

SERVES 4

- 1kg mixed wild mushrooms, torn into roughly even chunks
- olive oil
- 1 large onion, finely chopped
- 5 garlic cloves, minced
- 100ml dry white wine
- 250g cooked Puy lentils
- 1 tbsp miso paste
- 400ml vegetable stock
- 100ml double cream
- 1 tbsp cornflour, mixed with 1 tbsp water to make a slurry
- handful of parsley, leaves picked and finely chopped
- 3–4 medium floury potatoes, very finely sliced (with a mandoline if possible)
- salt and freshly ground black pepper

Preheat the oven to 180°C fan/390°F/gas 6.

Heat a dry, large ovenproof frying or sauté pan over a medium–high heat. Once hot, add half the mushrooms and a good pinch of salt and fry for 8–10 minutes, pushing them down into the pan to get some colour on them, until they are golden and have halved in size. Try not to stir them too much here, just let them do their thing. Remove from the pan and set aside. Repeat with the other half of the mushrooms, removing them from the pan and setting aside once they've cooked.

Next, heat a good glug of olive oil in the same pan set over a medium heat. Once hot, fry the onion for 6–8 minutes, stirring regularly, until soft and translucent. Add the garlic and fry for a further minute or so, just to soften.

Increase the heat to high and pour in the wine. Allow it to simmer and bubble for a minute or so, until almost evaporated. Return the heat back to medium and add the lentils, miso, vegetable stock and cream. Stir well, then whisk in the cornflour slurry. Bring to a gentle simmer, then reduce the heat slightly and cook for 6–8 minutes, stirring regularly, until the filling is thick and glossy. Stir through the mushrooms and parsley, then taste and adjust the seasoning, if needed.

Remove the pan from the heat and lay the slices of potato over the filling in an overlapping spiral pattern. I slice up three potatoes to begin with, see how far I get with those, then slice up the extra potato if I need it. They need to be sliced very finely to cook all the way through.

Brush the potato with olive oil and sprinkle over a pinch of salt and black pepper. Bake for 45–55 minutes, or until the potatoes are golden and soft all the way through. Allow the hotpot to sit for 5 minutes before serving in the middle of the table and letting everyone help themselves.

Miso Butter Jacket Potatoes

There is an ongoing joke in my house that whenever we are discussing what to have for dinner, I suggest a jacket potato. The joke started partly because James can't stand jacket potatoes (years of military lunches), but I adore them. I like the classic beans and cheese. But you don't need a recipe for that. This is my second favourite way to enjoy them. He will happily eat it too.

Chilli crisp oil can be very hot, so adapt as you need.

Preheat the oven to 200°C fan/425°F/gas 7.

First of all, we need to make the perfect jacket potato. Prick each potato a few times with a fork, then rub them all over with a glug of olive oil and a pinch of flaky salt. Place them directly on the shelf of your oven and cook for 1 hour–1 hour 15 minutes, turning them over halfway through, until they are crisp on the outside and can be easily pierced with a knife. Very large potatoes might need slightly longer than this; just keep an eye on them.

Meanwhile, combine the butter and miso paste in a small bowl and set aside.

Just before the potatoes are due out of the oven, heat a glug of olive oil in a small frying pan over a low–medium heat. Once hot, add the seeds and fry for 2–3 minutes, stirring constantly, until golden brown and toasted. They might pop and splutter, so stand back a bit. Remove from the heat, then stir through the chilli crisp and a pinch of salt.

Pierce open the jacket potatoes and fluff them up with a fork. Divide the miso butter between them, then top with a few good spoonfuls of kimchi and the chilli crisp seeds. Finish with a few coriander leaves and a sprinkling of flaky salt, if you like.

SERVES 2

- 2 large floury potatoes (I like King Edwards, but Maris Pipers are good too)
- olive oil
- 50g unsalted butter, at room temperature
- 1 tbsp white miso paste
- 20g mixed seeds (I use a mixture of pumpkin, sunflower and sesame)
- 2 tsp chilli crisp oil
- 3 tbsp kimchi
- small handful of coriander, leaves picked
- flaky salt

Cavolo Nero Orzo

You may know this hearty green with blistered leaves as Tuscan kale, or as black kale. To me, it has always been cavolo nero. I love the splash of colour it brings to an autumn colour palette.

You can use this recipe as a template to transcend the seasons. Swap the cavolo nero for spinach in spring and early summer and for curly kale in the winter. The method will remain the same.

Melt half the butter in a large frying pan over a medium heat. Add all the cavolo nero and a pinch of salt and fry for 3–4 minutes, stirring regularly, until bright green and slightly wilted. Combine the wilted cavolo nero, lemon juice and 100ml of the stock in a high-powered blender and blend until mostly smooth. If your blender is struggling, you can add a dash more of the stock to help it along. Set aside.

Wipe out your pan and return it to a medium heat. Add a good glug of olive oil and once hot, fry the onion and a pinch of salt for 6–8 minutes, until soft and translucent. Add the garlic and fry for a further minute or so, just to soften. Stir through the orzo, to coat it in the oil.

Add a ladleful of the hot stock to the orzo and stir continuously. Once all the stock has been absorbed into the orzo, add another ladleful of stock. Repeat this step, stirring continuously between ladlefuls, until the orzo is tender and creamy. If you find your orzo is still too al dente after using up all your stock, you can add another ladleful of liquid – either make up a little more stock or use boiling water. I like my orzo quite loose, so I'll add an extra dash of water here, if I need to.

Remove the pan from the heat and stir through the cavolo nero purée and the remaining butter, watching the orzo turn a rich green as you do. Grind in a little black pepper, then taste and adjust the seasoning and the lemon juice, if needed.

Serve the orzo between plates or shallow bowls and swirl over your best extra virgin olive oil. It doesn't need anything else. I think it's quite chic serving a dish so simply, letting the cavolo nero take centre stage. But if you fancy it, a spoonful of ricotta and a grating of lemon zest are pleasing additions.

SERVES 2

30g unsalted butter
200g cavolo nero, hard stems removed, roughly chopped
juice of ½ lemon, plus a little extra to serve
800ml hot vegetable stock
olive oil
1 small onion, finely chopped
2 garlic cloves, minced
225g orzo pasta
salt and freshly ground black pepper

TO SERVE
extra virgin olive oil
ricotta
a little grated lemon zest

Wild Mushrooms & Pickled Walnuts with Cheesy Polenta

Autumn is the season for wild mushrooms in the UK, because the cooler, wetter weather helps their fruiting bodies to flourish. I'm not confident enough to forage for wild mushrooms without an expert, so I buy mine from the grocer. You can find a great selection of fungi in the supermarkets now too. It's nice to use a variety here if you can – shapes, textures, sizes. Whatever you can find.

Start by making the polenta. Bring the milk, 500ml of water and a good pinch of salt to a boil in a large saucepan. It will boil over if you leave it too long, so just keep an eye on it. Reduce the heat to low, then, whisking as you go, gradually add the polenta until it is smooth and combined. Simmer the polenta, whisking regularly, for 25–35 minutes, or until it's thick, fluffy and no longer sticks to the bottom of the pan (if you're using quick cook polenta, it will only need 4–5 minutes of cooking, so you can make it right before serving). Remove the pan from the heat and stir through the butter, Parmesan, Cheddar and lots of pepper until melted. Taste and adjust the seasoning, if needed.

Meanwhile, heat a large dry frying pan over a medium–high heat. Once hot, add the mushrooms and a good pinch of salt and fry for 4–6 minutes, pushing them down into the pan to get some colour on them, until they are lightly golden and releasing their liquid. Try not to stir them too much here, just let them do their thing.

Add a glug of olive oil, the pickled walnuts, garlic, rosemary, and a pinch of salt to the pan and stir well to combine. Fry for a further 2–3 minutes, stirring frequently, until the garlic is soft and golden. Increase the heat to high and pour in the wine. Let it bubble and simmer for a minute or so, until completely reduced. Remove the pan from the heat, pop on the lid and let it sit while the polenta finishes cooking.

Ladle the cheesy, creamy polenta into shallow bowls and spoon over the mushrooms and any juices left in the pan. Finish with another grating of Parmesan and a good crack of black pepper.

SERVES 2

- 125ml milk
- 80g polenta
- 25g unsalted butter
- 25g Parmesan, finely grated
- 50g extra mature Cheddar, grated
- 400g mixed wild mushrooms, torn into roughly even chunks
- olive oil
- 100g pickled walnuts, drained and roughly chopped
- 3 garlic cloves, thinly sliced
- 1 sprig of rosemary, leaves picked
- 75ml dry white wine
- salt and freshly ground black pepper

A Gorgeous Pumpkin Curry

There is a little village called Slindon close to where I grew up. Every October, since 1968, a man called Ralph Upton hosted a pumpkin festival, displaying and selling the pumpkins he grew in his own fields. You could buy over 80 varieties there; it was quite incredible. Every year he would create a giant mosaic from the pumpkins too – pictures of spitfires, tractors, butterflies. If you have a chance to look it up, do.

I met Ralph several times, before he passed away in 2009. He introduced me to many varieties of squash, including Delica, which is used here. It roasts up to a rich honeyed sweetness and pairs wonderfully with the curry sauce, which is a nod to lubya, the rich Afghan curry.

Delica pumpkins are also known as Kabocha squash or Japanese pumpkin (see page 162 for more squash/pumpkin info). If you can't get your hands on one, I would substitute it with Red Kuri, or Crown Prince. (See photo overleaf.)

SERVES 4

1 medium Delica pumpkin, skin left on, deseeded and quartered
neutral oil
1 onion, finely chopped
4 garlic cloves, minced
1 red chilli, deseeded and finely chopped
4 tbsp tomato purée
2 tsp coriander seeds
1 tsp cumin seeds
2 tsp dried mint
400g tin plum tomatoes
200g tin kidney beans, drained and rinsed
750ml vegetable stock
1 tbsp red wine vinegar
salt and freshly ground black pepper
rice or naan breads, to serve

PINK PICKLED ONIONS
½ red onion, very finely sliced
juice of 1 lemon

Preheat the oven to 160°C fan/350°F/gas 4.

Combine the Delica pumpkin with a good glug of neutral oil and a pinch of salt and black pepper on a large baking tray. Use your hands to give everything a good mix and rub the oil into the flesh and skin. Roast for 45–50 minutes, turning once halfway through, until golden and deeply caramelized on the edges.

Meanwhile, make the pink pickled onions. Combine the sliced red onion, lemon juice and a good pinch of salt in a small bowl. Use your fingers to massage them together for a minute or so, until the onions have softened and are turning pink. Set them to one side and let them macerate while you continue with the recipe.

Next, heat a large saucepan over a medium heat and add a good glug of neutral oil. Once hot, add the onion and a pinch of salt and fry for 6–8 minutes, until soft and translucent. Add the garlic, red chilli, tomato purée, coriander seeds, cumin seeds and dried mint and fry for a further 2–3 minutes, until the garlic is soft and the tomato purée has darkened in colour.

Recipe continues overleaf

Pour in the plum tomatoes and season with a good pinch of salt and black pepper. Use the back of your wooden spoon to roughly mash the plum tomatoes into the base of the pan, then stir through the kidney beans and vegetable stock. Bring everything to a gentle simmer, then reduce the heat to low and cook for 20–25 minutes, stirring regularly, until the sauce has reduced and the kidney beans are really tender. Remove from the heat and use a hand blender to blitz it into a silky smooth sauce, adding a little extra stock, or water, if it's too thick. It should be pourable and have the consistency of soup. You could also blend this in a stand blender, just let it cool down slightly first. Stir through the red wine vinegar, then taste and adjust the seasoning, if needed.

Ladle the sauce between plates and top each one with a quarter of the roasted pumpkin. Finish with a few pink pickled onions and a crack of black pepper. Serve with rice or naan breads, if you like. It's a gorgeous dish.

Beetroot Velvet Cake

I think there needs to be a good reason to add vegetables to a cake. I doubt it makes it any better for us (although I think a slice of cake is a great thing – it soothes the soul). So most of the time, it is to inject extra moisture. This beetroot velvet cake is most certainly moist. It has a depth to it too, so difficult to find in cakes. It's one of James's favourite things I bake.

I don't think it needs to be a special occasion to make a cake look gorgeous. Life is always worth celebrating. But if you are celebrating for something particularly special, you could ice the whole of the outside, marbling a little purple food colouring through the icing if you like. If you are short on time, this cake is still lovely iced simply, without the marbling, as shown in the photos overleaf. You can also halve the icing ingredients and spread it only in the middle, if that's how you prefer it.

SERVES 10

240g raw beetroot (about 3–4), weighed after topping and tailing
2 tbsp apple cider vinegar
240ml milk
400g caster sugar
pinch of salt
110ml neutral oil
2 tsp vanilla extract
215g plain flour
85g cocoa powder
1 tsp baking powder
2 tsp bicarbonate of soda

CREAM CHEESE ICING
280g full-fat cream cheese, at room temperature
150g unsalted butter, at room temperature
2 tsp vanilla extract
400g icing sugar

Preheat the oven to 180°C fan/390°F/gas 6.

Scrub the beetroots under running water until they are clean and bright purple. Fold them into a tight parcel of baking parchment or tin foil (this helps them to steam as they bake), then place on a baking tray and bake for 1 hour 15 minutes– 1 hour 30 minutes, or until the beetroot can be pierced easily with a knife. Leave them to cool.

Lower the oven to 160°C fan/350°F/gas 4 and grease and/or line two 20cm baking tins (slightly larger or smaller ones will also work).

Combine the baked beetroot (and any liquid left in its parcel), apple cider vinegar and milk in a high-powered blender and blend until smooth and silky. Pour the mixture into a mixing bowl and stir through the sugar, salt, oil and vanilla extract.

Sift the plain flour, cocoa powder, baking powder and bicarbonate of soda into the wet ingredients. Gently fold everything together, until you have a glossy, lump-free batter. Divide evenly between the two baking tins (you can weigh them out if you like, but I never bother) and bake for 25–35 minutes, or until a skewer inserted into the centre comes out clean. Let the cakes sit for 15 minutes, before turning out onto a wire rack to cool. They are fragile! So be careful.

While the cakes are baking, make the cream cheese icing. First, make sure both your cream cheese and your butter are fully at room temperature. It is very important! Combine in a mixing bowl and use an electric whisk to beat until creamy and lighter in colour. Add the vanilla extract and whisk that in too. Next, sift the icing sugar into the bowl and fold gently into the mixture. Using the electric whisk again, beat the icing for 2–3 minutes, until thick, smooth and silky. Refrigerate the icing while the cake is cooking and cooling.

Once the cakes have cooled fully, sandwich them with the cream cheese icing and use an off-set spatula or a palette knife to smooth it on top or over the top and sides (it doesn't need to be perfect; I think rustic cakes are better anyway).

Cut into slices and share with your favourite people. You'll need to keep it refrigerated if saving overnight. It will keep for a few days.

Ripe Figs, Honey Mascarpone & Pistachio Brittle

This is the best way to showcase figs in all their glory: tearing them open to expose their speckled flesh. Muted greens and deep purples. You'll end up with leftover brittle; a completely wonderful thing. Keep it in an airtight container and nibble on it throughout the week. Also, if you can get your hands on lavender honey, absolutely use that here. Its subtle floral undertones are gorgeous with the figs.

Begin by making the pistachio brittle. Combine the butter, golden caster sugar, golden syrup and 2 teaspoons of water in a medium saucepan. Place over a low-medium heat and stir for 2–3 minutes, until the sugar has dissolved and the mixture is combined.

Increase the heat slightly and bring the pan to a boil. Boil the mixture for 4–5 minutes, stirring occasionally, or until the mixture is a rich amber colour. Watch it carefully here. It can turn from golden to burnt in a matter of seconds.

Remove the pan from the heat and stir through the pistachios, until the caramel is silky and glossy. Pour the mixture out onto a lined baking tray and quickly spread it into one thin even layer. Be careful not to get the mixture on your fingers – it's molten sugar! Let it sit for 20 minutes, to harden.

Next, combine the mascarpone with the honey in a small bowl. Whisk until smooth and combined. Refrigerate until ready to serve.

To serve, tear open your figs and serve two on each plate. Generously dollop with the mascarpone, then slice your pistachio brittle into shards and serve a few with each plate. Finish with a small pinch of flaky salt, if you like.

SERVES 4

PISTACHIO BRITTLE
60g salted butter
90g golden caster sugar
100g golden syrup
100g shelled pistachios

TO SERVE
200g mascarpone
1 tbsp runny honey
8 large ripe figs
flaky salt

Rice Pudding & Jammy Figs

My mum was never a huge fan of cooking. She used to say that having children made her resent cooking as all we wanted was simple beige food. I think that might have been an excuse, however, as my dad can't remember her ever being enthused by the thought of cooking. But the food she did make for me was fantastic. Dishes her mother passed down to her, which now, she has passed on to me. Stew with extra dumplings, Victoria sponge, macaroni cheese and rice pudding – which was always made in the oven, rather than on the stove, just as I've done here. We would eat it with a spoonful of strawberry jam, sitting in front of the TV, mother and daughter. I like to think that she would have liked this version too; with cardamom, vanilla and jammy figs.

(See photos overleaf.)

Preheat the oven to 140°C fan/320°F/gas 3, and lightly grease a baking dish with the butter. My baking dish is roughly 20 x 25cm in size but one slightly bigger or smaller will work.

Crush the cardamom pods with the side of a knife and combine in a large saucepan with the milk, double cream, vanilla seeds and remaining pod and a pinch of salt. Place over a medium heat and gently warm, stirring regularly, until the liquid is almost coming to a boil. Remove from the heat.

Combine the pudding rice and caster sugar in the greased baking dish and pour over the hot milk, along with the cardamom and vanilla pods. Give everything a quick stir, then bake for 1 hour 15 minutes–1 hour 45 minutes, or until a golden skin has formed on top and the rice is tender underneath. Remove from the oven and let the pudding stand for 5 minutes.

Meanwhile, make the jammy figs. Combine the figs, granulated sugar and 75ml water in a saucepan. Give them a good stir, then bring everything to a boil over a medium-high heat. Reduce the heat to a gentle simmer and cook for 20–25 minutes, stirring occasionally, until the figs are jammy and falling apart. Any liquid left in the pan will thicken into a lovely syrup as it cools.

Serve the hot rice pudding generously in big bowls, picking out the cardamom and vanilla pods as you do. Top with the jammy figs and spoonfuls of their gorgeous syrup.

SERVES 4

unsalted butter, for greasing
8 cardamom pods
800ml milk
150ml double cream
1 vanilla pod, sliced down the middle and seeds scraped out
pinch of salt
130g pudding rice
3 tbsp caster sugar

JAMMY FIGS
8 figs, hard tops trimmed, quartered
100g granulated sugar

Apple & Ginger Tarte Tatin

If tarte tatin is on the menu, I'll be ordering it. The sticky sweet apples, crunchy puff pastry. It's also a favourite one to make. Watching the sugar bubble into a golden caramel, like magic. Tarte tatin is a deceivingly easy dessert to make, it's all about practice. Take it off the heat when you see the caramel turn a golden amber – the colour of honey. Make a few of them and you'll have it mastered. I think of the ginger crème fraiche as essential – a sharp antidote to the luscious caramel.

~~~~~~~~~~~~~~~~

Roll the block of puff pastry out to a 3–4mm thickness. Cut a circle of the pastry the same size as the top rim of a medium ovenproof frying pan. I use a 25cm diameter cast iron pan, but you'll be fine with one slightly larger too. Refrigerate the pastry circle while you continue with the recipe.

Sprinkle the caster sugar into the base of the same pan, then dot the butter over the top. Arrange the apples on top, overlapping them to fit them all in, if needed, their rounded sides facing into the sugar.

Heat the oven to 180°C fan/390°F/gas 6.

Place the pan over a low-medium heat, letting it sit undisturbed for 12–15 minutes, or until the sugar has caramelized and is golden amber in colour. Watch the pan carefully here, as the sugar can turn from amber to dark and burnt in a matter of minutes. You also want to make sure it's caramelizing evenly, moving the pan around the stove if it's browning quicker in spots. Remove from the heat, then grate the fresh ginger over the top of the apples. Sprinkle the ground ginger over the apples too. Quickly cover it with the chilled puff pastry circle, tucking it in around the edges. Prick the pastry several times with a knife, then bake for 25–30 minutes, or until puffed and golden.

Meanwhile you can make the ginger crème fraiche. Combine the crème fraiche, chopped stem ginger and the syrup in a bowl. Give everything a good stir, then refrigerate until you are ready to eat.

Let the tarte Tatin cool for 5 minutes to give the caramel a chance to set. Run a knife around the outside of the pastry, before carefully turning it out onto a board. Cut it into generous slices and serve with a good dollop of the ginger crème fraiche on top.

SERVES 6

300g puff pastry block
150g caster sugar
125g unsalted butter, cubed
6 eating apples, peeled, cored and quartered
½ a thumb-sized piece ginger, peeled
1 generous tsp ground ginger

GINGER CRÈME FRAICHE

200g crème fraiche
2 balls stem ginger in syrup, plus two tbsp of its syrup

Blackberry Old Fashioned

A cocktail of quiet indulgence, where a flavour that dances between sweet and earthy meets the smooth warmth of bourbon. A few dashes of bitters pulls it all into balance – simple, yet sublime.

You'll probably have leftover blackberry syrup here; not a bad thing at all. It's very nice stirred through plain yoghurt, or drizzled over vanilla ice cream. You can use it as a cordial for soda water or lemonade, too.

Start by making the blackberry simple syrup. Combine the blackberries, caster sugar and 85ml of water in a small saucepan. Place over a medium heat and bring to a simmer, stirring frequently. Lower the heat slightly, and cook for 5–6 minutes, using the back of your spoon to mash the blackberries as you stir, until you have a bright purple purée.

Strain the blackberry mixture through a fine mesh sieve into a jug, using the back of your spoon to help it through, if needed. (Enjoy the mashed blackberries as they are, or with a bowl of yoghurt.) Let the blackberry simple syrup cool completely, then you're ready to make your cocktail.

Combine 2 teaspoons of the blackberry simple syrup, bourbon/rye whiskey, Angostura bitters and a handful of ice in a jug. Stir until the outside of the jug is ice cold, then strain into a rocks glass containing one large ice cube. Garnish with a few blackberries, if you like.

MAKES 1, WITH LEFTOVER SIMPLE SYRUP

2 shots bourbon or rye whiskey
3 dashes Angostura bitters
fresh blackberries, to garnish

BLACKBERRY SIMPLE SYRUP
80g blackberries
80g caster sugar

WINTER

Shorter days, colder weather and darker evenings influence both my mood and how I cook. I want dishes to warm and comfort me, and so nature follows suit with leeks and celeriac, cauliflower and parsnips. There are some recipes with a lengthier process in this chapter – making pastry, peeling Jerusalem artichokes – because winter is a time to lean into the joys of slow cooking; taking solace in your cosy kitchen when it is too cold to go outside. I make the most of the speckles of vibrancy coming from blood oranges, radicchio, pomegranate and kale, all peeking through the whites and browns of winter.

EARLY WINTER

Apple

Pear

Citrus (orange, clementine, tangerine and satsuma)

Beetroot

Carrot

Celeriac

Celery

Chard

Chicory

Kale

Cavolo nero

Leek

Swede

Turnip

Winter squash

Brussels sprout

Cabbage

Jerusalem artichoke

Parsnip

Potato

Cauliflower

LATE WINTER

Rhubarb (forced)

Apple

Pear

Citrus (orange, clementine, tangerine and satsuma)

Beetroot

Carrot

Celeriac

Celery

Purple sprouting broccoli

Chicory

Kale

Cavolo nero

Leek

Swede

Turnip

Winter squash

Brussels sprout

Cabbage

Jerusalem artichoke

Parsnip

Potato

Sprout, Sticky Onion & Chestnut Toast

My top three carbohydrates, when listed from 1–3, would be: bread, then bread, then bread. It is one of life's greatest, most simple pleasures and truthfully, it saddens me when I am told someone can't (or won't) eat it. Most days I'll find a way to slot it into one of my meals, and when Christmas is around the corner, I lean towards this. Shredded sprouts, fried until dark around the edges for bags of flavour, sweet sticky onions and cool, creamy burrata. It's a welcome contrast from the more traditional festive food, I think.

MAKES 2 SLICES

olive oil
1 small onion, finely sliced
1 tbsp brown sugar
1 tbsp balsamic vinegar
200g Brussels sprouts, trimmed and finely sliced
50g cooked chestnuts, roughly chopped
150g ball of burrata
2 slices crusty bread, toasted
salt and freshly ground black pepper

TO SERVE

toasted hazelnuts, roughly chopped
lemon wedges

Heat a medium frying pan over a low–medium heat and add a good glug of oil. Once hot, add the sliced onion and a good pinch of salt and cook gently for 12–15 minutes, stirring regularly and lowering the heat if they begin to catch. Cook until the onion is soft and beginning to caramelize. Add the sugar and balsamic vinegar and continue to cook for a further 3–5 minutes, or until the onion is lovely and sticky. Remove from the pan and set aside.

Heat another glug of oil in the same pan set over a medium-high heat. Once hot, add the Brussels sprouts, chestnuts and a pinch of salt and fry, stirring frequently, for 6–8 minutes, until the sprouts are beginning to char. Stir through the sticky onions, then taste and adjust the seasoning, if needed.

Whisk up the burrata with a fork and spread generously over the toast. Spoon the sprout mixture on top, then finish with a few chopped toasted hazelnuts and a good crack of black pepper. Serve with a wedge of lemon on the side.

Bruschetta with Maple Pears & Thyme Ricotta

My dad inherited a wonderfully fruitful garden from the previous owners of the house I partly grew up in. We were not so green-fingered ourselves, so most of the garden was left to fend for itself, including the fruit trees: apple – both cooking and eating – greengage and pear. We had a hammock strung up between the cooking apple and pear tree, and I spent many a happy afternoon swinging in our wild garden, chomping on a not-quite-ripe conference pear. They have remained a favourite of mine ever since.

This bruschetta walks the line between sweet and savoury. One of my favourite ways to eat. You'll want to use a firm pear here; a firm Conference or a Bosc would be my choice.

(See photo overleaf.)

SERVES 2

- olive oil
- 2 firm pears, quartered and seeds removed
- 1 tbsp maple syrup
- 150g ricotta
- 4 sprigs of thyme, leaves picked and finely chopped, plus extra leaves to serve
- 1 tbsp milk
- 2 large slices rye sourdough bread
- walnuts, very thinly sliced
- salt and freshly ground black pepper

Preheat the oven to 180°C fan/390°F/gas 4.

Heat a griddle pan over a high heat and brush with olive oil. Once hot, add the sliced pear and griddle for 2–3 minutes on each cut side, or until grilled with dark char marks.

Transfer the pears to a small baking dish and add the maple syrup, a drizzle of olive oil and a good pinch of salt and black pepper. Use your hands to give everything a mix, then bake for 10–15 minutes, or until the pears are tender but still hold their shape.

Next, combine the ricotta, thyme, milk, a good pinch of salt and a few really generous grinds of pepper in a bowl. Give everything a good mix, then taste and adjust the seasoning, if needed.

Toast the bread in the griddle pan (you could also do this in the toaster, but while the griddle pan is out, you might as well use it). Spread generously with the ricotta, then layer over the pears and drizzle with any juice left from their baking tray. Finish with an extra sprinkling of thyme, the sliced walnuts, a pinch of flaky salt and a good crack of black pepper.

Five Spice Kalettes & Peanut Dip

My first time living away from home was with my friend Charlotte. We rented a little apartment close to the beach and had a beautiful few years there. Over the Covid lockdown, Charlotte and I spent our New Year's Eve as a three with our friend and next-door neighbour, Toby. He made roasted kalettes (kale sprouts) sprinkled with five spice as a little end-of-year nibble for us and carried them on their baking tray the five steps from his apartment. I believe they were an idea and creation of his own.

    I attended Charlotte and Toby's wedding last year. Was it fate? Or maybe it was the kalettes? We will never know. I still like to think of this as a lucky dish though. A starter at the start of a love story.

SERVES 4, AS A NIBBLE

400g kalettes
2 generous tsp Chinese five spice
sesame oil
salt

PEANUT DIP
3 tbsp smooth peanut butter
1½ tbsp soy sauce
1 tbsp brown sugar
juice of ½ lime
½ thumb-sized piece ginger, grated

Preheat the oven to 180°C fan/390°F/gas 6.

    Combine the kalettes, Chinese five spice, a really good drizzle of sesame oil and a generous pinch of salt in a mixing bowl. Use your hands to give everything a toss, to coat the kalettes in the oily spices.

    Pour the kalettes out onto a large baking tray, or between two smaller ones. We want them all to have their own space, not to be touching one another. Roast for 10–15 minutes, or until the outside leaves of the kalettes are crispy.

    While the kalettes are roasting, you can make the dipping sauce. Combine the peanut butter, soy sauce, brown sugar, lime juice and grated ginger in a bowl. Add 2 tablespoons of cold water, then whisk until smooth and combined, adding more water to loosen it, if needed. It should be silky and shiny and easily drop off a spoon. Taste and add a pinch of salt, if you think it needs it.

    Pour the dipping sauce into a small serving bowl and pile up the roasted kalettes around it. Dip and dip until the kalettes are gone, then make another batch.

Chicory, Pears & Candied Thyme Walnuts

This recipe gives you two choices. You can eat it as a fresh wintery salad, but it is also very nice served as little cups, to nibble on with a drink in the festive period (as photographed here, see overleaf). It's a beautiful combination: the bitter chicory balanced by the sugared walnuts. I use a vegetarian pecorino here, ideally one that is made in Yorkshire. It's creamy, nutty and delicate and worth hunting down.

You'll struggle to make the small leaves at the centre of the chicory into the little cups, so I don't bother. Instead, I'll just dip them into the dressing and nibble on them as I cook. A chef's treat, if you will.

~~~~~~~~~~~~~~~~~~~

Start by making the dressing. Combine the Dijon mustard, red wine vinegar, extra virgin olive oil, chopped shallot and a good pinch of salt and black pepper in a small jug. Give everything a good stir to combine, then taste and adjust the seasoning, if needed. Let it sit and macerate while you continue with the recipe.

Next, make the candied walnuts. Combine the walnuts, caster sugar, butter and thyme in a small frying pan. Place over a low–medium heat and stir frequently for 4–5 minutes, or until the sugar turns from grainy to silky smooth and is coating the nuts. Quickly pour them out onto a lined baking tray and use two forks to separate each one, so they don't stick together. Keep your fingers away from them here. It's molten sugar! Set them aside for 10 minutes, to let them harden.

Now, you have two options. To make this into a salad, layer the chicory leaves, pecorino, pear and a few spoonfuls of dressing in a serving dish. Chop up the candied walnuts, sprinkle them over the top and finish with a pinch of flaky salt and a good crack of black pepper. Or, to make these into cute bite-sized nibbles/canapés, take each chicory leaf and layer a slice of pear, a slice of pecorino, a little of the dressing and one candied walnut within its curves. Finish each one with a pinch of flaky salt and a grind of black pepper, then arrange on a serving plate. They are particularly lovely with a glass of Pinot Gris.

SERVES 4 AS A NIBBLE,
OR 2 AS A SALAD

50g walnut halves
30g caster sugar
10g salted butter
2 sprigs of thyme, leaves picked
3 red chicory, ends trimmed and leaves separated
50g pecorino, thinly sliced
1 firm pear, thinly sliced
salt and freshly ground black pepper

DRESSING
1 tsp Dijon mustard
1 tbsp red wine vinegar
2 tbsp extra virgin olive oil
1 round shallot, finely chopped

Zesty Kale Salad

This is a very simple recipe – so much so, I almost didn't include it in the book. Really, it's a recipe to complement and contrast others. Cooking is about balancing and the better you can balance, the better cook you'll become. A hearty winter dish can so often need something bright and zingy to lift it, which is exactly where this kale salad excels. I'll eat it with almost anything in this chapter – try it with the Cauliflower Gnocchi Cheese Bake on page 259, or the Leek, Thyme & Butter Bean Gratin on page 243.

SERVES 4, AS A SIDE

juice and zest of 1 lemon
1 small garlic clove, grated
1 tsp Dijon mustard
½ tsp runny honey
3 tbsp extra virgin olive oil
400g kale, hard stems removed, roughly chopped
salt and freshly ground black pepper

Combine the lemon zest and juice, garlic, Dijon mustard, honey, extra virgin olive oil and a good pinch of salt and black pepper in a bowl. Whisk until smooth and combined, then taste and adjust the seasoning, if needed.

In a large mixing bowl, combine the kale and one third of the dressing. Use your hands to scrunch and massage the dressing into the kale for 3–4 minutes, until the kale has darkened in colour and halved in size. Don't skimp on this step – massaging the kale softens its fibres, making it far more pleasant to eat.

Stir the remaining dressing through the kale, then taste and adjust the seasoning, if needed. Serve it as the base of a salad, or on its own as a side dish – however you wish.

Persimmon, Burrata & Chilli Crisp

Rather than a recipe, you could say this is more a collection of delicious ingredients. A ball of dreamy, creamy burrata, frozen shaved persimmon and a good drizzle of chilli crisp. Three beautiful ingredients that work beautifully together. What's wrong with that?

We are freezing the persimmon for two reasons here: one, it allows you to grate it into a fine dust, which you wouldn't be able to achieve otherwise. And two, the contrast you achieve between the ice-cold persimmon and the fiery heat of the chilli crisp is a surprise to the senses, in the best possible way.

(See photos overleaf.)

~~~~~~~~~~~~~~~~~~

This recipe starts the night before, or at least 3 hours before, as you need to freeze the persimmon until completely solid.

About 15 minutes before you are ready to serve, take the burrata out of the fridge and leave it at room temperature, to warm up a little.

Break the burrata apart on a pretty plate. Use a fine grater (I use a Microplane) to grate over roughly half of the frozen persimmon (the rest you can put back in the freezer for another time), then drizzle over a spoonful or two of chilli crisp.

Finish with a good sprinkling of flaky salt, then serve immediately with lots of crusty bread to dip and scoop.

SERVES 2

1 persimmon
150g ball of burrata
chilli crisp oil
flaky salt
really nice bread, to serve

Crispy Pan-fried Jerusalem Artichokes

Jerusalem artichokes are quirky little roots with their knobbly gnarled exterior and sweet, nutty flesh. They make a welcome wintery change to crispy potatoes.

In this recipe you crush the Jerusalem artichokes a little before frying, pressing them down just enough to split their skins, increasing their surface area – extra room for crispiness! The outside fries to a golden, caramelized crust, while the soft, nutty flesh inside stays tender and sweet. A sprinkle of sea salt, a hint of rosemary. Heavenly stuff.

Bring a large pan of salted water to the boil. Add the Jerusalem artichokes, then bring the pan back to a boil. Cook for 10–12 minutes, or until the Jerusalem artichokes are easily pierced with a knife, but are still holding their shape. Drain and let them steam dry. Then, crush each one with a spatula on a chopping board, so its skin bursts and it lays flat.

Next, heat a large frying pan over a medium heat and add enough olive oil to coat the bottom. Once hot, add one of the rosemary sprigs, a few of the flattened Jerusalem artichokes (being careful not to overcrowd the pan), and a good pinch of salt and fry for 4–5 minutes each side, or until darkly golden and crisp. Repeat with the remaining Jerusalem artichokes, frying them in batches and adding extra rosemary and oil as needed.

Sprinkle the crisp Jerusalem artichokes with flaky salt, then serve as you would potatoes: as a side dish, on their own with a good mayonnaise (my preference), with a roast dinner. It's up to you.

SERVES 4, AS A SIDE

500g Jerusalem artichokes, skins scrubbed
olive oil
a few sprigs of rosemary
salt

Very Untraditional French Onion Soup

French onion soup is a perfect example of how with time and care, a thing as humble and unassuming as the onion can be transformed into something magical. It's a dish that can't be rushed; the low and uber-slow cooking of the onion is the key to creating depth in this deep, dark bowl of soup. Now, I can't claim my version to be traditional at all, hence the name. But it is how I like it. Slightly brothier than the original, with added beans and winter greens. Most often I'll eat this just on its own, cosied up on the sofa, letting it warm and soothe me from the outside in. Although, a slice of cheese on toast on the side can never hurt.

SERVES 4

60g unsalted butter
6 large onions, finely sliced (use a mandoline if you have one, it's much quicker)
1½ tbsp brown sugar
1 tbsp balsamic vinegar
200ml dry white wine
2 litres really good quality vegetable stock
3 tbsp soy sauce
2 bay leaves
4 sprigs of thyme
400g jar butter beans, drained and rinsed
2 large handfuls of kale, hard stems removed, roughly chopped
salt and freshly ground black pepper

Melt the butter in a large heavy-bottomed pan over medium-high heat. Add the onions and a really good pinch of salt and fry, stirring frequently, for 2–3 minutes to get them started. It will look like a lot of onions, but they will greatly reduce. Reduce the heat to low, cover the pan with a lid and cook for 10–12 minutes, stirring occasionally, until the onions are soft.

Sprinkle the brown sugar and balsamic vinegar over the onions, stir well and continue to cook, uncovered this time, for 30–35 minutes, stirring regularly and reducing the heat if they begin to catch at any point. Watch as the onion changes slowly from a pale yellow to an earthy gold.

Increase the heat to medium, pour in the wine and allow to simmer and bubble for 2–3 minutes, until almost completely evaporated. Then add the stock, soy sauce, bay leaves and thyme. Bring everything to a boil and cook for 8–10 minutes, or until the stock has reduced and the onion is buttery-soft.

Finally, stir through the beans and kale, until the kale has wilted. Taste and adjust the seasoning, if needed.

Remove the bay leaves and thyme sprigs from the soup, then ladle liberally into bowls. Serve as it is, or with a slice of cheese on toast, if you fancy.

Celeriac & Spelt Soup
(with lots of crispy sage)

Celeriac should be a regular on our home menus. Thanks to its knobbly, alien-like exterior, it's known as the ugly duckling of vegetables, but I see it more as a swan – the distinct flavour of its nutty white flesh somewhere between celery and a potato, with the texture of a parsnip.

Despite appearances, celeriac is easy to prep. Use a speed peeler to peel off the rough skin and the tangle of roots, until you reach the white flesh underneath. Any dirt can simply be washed or brushed off.

~~~~~~~~~~~~~~~~

Heat a good glug of olive oil in a large saucepan set over a medium heat. Once hot, fry the onion and a pinch of salt for 6–8 minutes, stirring regularly, until soft and translucent. Add the celeriac and continue to fry for a further 12–15 minutes, or until it has softened and is turning slightly golden. Stir through the chopped rosemary for a further minute or so, until it releases its fragrance.

Next, add the spelt, vegetable stock and a pinch of salt to the pan. Bring everything to a gentle simmer, then lower the heat slightly and cook for 35–40 minutes, stirring regularly, until both the celeriac and spelt are tender. Add the kale and stir for a few minutes, until it has wilted. Taste and adjust the seasoning, if needed.

Meanwhile, heat a really good glug of olive oil in a small frying pan over a medium–high heat. Once hot, add the sage leaves and fry for 20–30 seconds, until crisp. Use a slotted spoon to remove them from the oil and onto a sheet of kitchen towel, to soak up any excess grease.

Combine the crème fraiche, chopped chives and lemon zest in a small bowl. Season generously with salt and black pepper, then stir well. Taste and adjust the seasoning, if needed.

To serve, ladle the soup between bowls and top with a dollop of the crème fraiche and a few sage leaves. Finish with a drizzle of your best extra virgin olive oil and a good crack of black pepper.

SERVES 4

olive oil
2 onions, finely chopped
500g celeriac, peeled and chopped into small chunks
4 sprigs of rosemary, leaves picked and finely chopped
100g spelt
1.5 litres vegetable stock
3 handfuls of kale, hard stems removed
20 sage leaves
salt and freshly ground black pepper
extra virgin olive oil, to serve

LEMON & CHIVE CRÈME FRAICHE
100g crème fraiche
a few chives, finely chopped
zest of 1 lemon

Blood Orange & Radicchio Salad

SERVES 2

4 blood oranges, peeled, sliced into rounds and seeds removed
½ radicchio, core removed and leaves separated
small handful of mint, leaves picked
small handful of shelled roasted pistachios, roughly chopped
150g ball mozzarella, drained and torn into pieces
flaky salt and freshly ground black pepper

DRESSING

4 tbsp extra virgin olive oil
2 tbsp white wine vinegar
1 tsp wholegrain mustard
1 shallot, very finely sliced into rounds

A bloody gorgeous salad. A salad of contrasts too – sweet, sharp, bitter, fresh.

Beautiful radicchio is often overlooked. Its deep, tannic-like bitterness can be jarring at first. Yet, in the right context – like this one, where its complexity has a citrussy sweetness to bounce off – it's transformed.

Begin by making the dressing. Combine the olive oil, white wine vinegar, mustard and a good pinch of salt and black pepper in a small bowl. Taste and adjust the seasoning, if needed. Stir through the shallot, then let the dressing sit and macerate for 15 minutes.

Layer up the sliced blood oranges, radicchio, mint, pistachios and mozzarella, drizzling the dressing generously between the layers. Leftover dressing will last a few days in the fridge, if you have any. Finish with a good crack of black pepper and a sprinkling of flaky salt and you'll be ready to eat.

SPROUTS

10 WAYS WITH BRUSSELS SPROUTS

Brussels sprouts are divisive little things. Slightly bitter, mildly earthy. I love them, but for those who don't, I truly believe it is because you have never had them cooked as they deserve to be cooked. Below are 10 ways to celebrate the humble sprout.

You'll find Brussels sprouts at their best during the winter months. If you can find them still on their stalk, even better – they tend to be slightly fresher. To prep them, trim off the hard bottom and peel away any leaves that look a little tired. From here, you can keep them whole, halve them, shred them – whatever you, or your recipe, desires.

1 SIMPLY ROASTED

Trim and halve the sprouts, tossing them with a glug of olive oil and a good pinch of salt and black pepper. Pour out onto a baking tray and roast at 160°C fan/350°F/gas 4 for 20–30 minutes, stirring halfway through, until tender in the middle and crisp and golden at the edges. You can leave it here, or as I like to do, finish them with a squeeze of lemon juice and a good grating of Parmesan.

2 RAW BRUSSELS SALAD

Trim 300g sprouts, and slice them as finely as you can with a mandoline. Combine them in a mixing bowl with a good glug of extra virgin olive oil, juice of ½ lemon, 1 tbsp sherry vinegar, 1 tsp wholegrain mustard and a good pinch of salt and black pepper. Give everything a stir, then cover and set aside to macerate for 15–20 minutes. To serve, stir 1 finely chopped apple, a handful of toasted chopped pecans and 40g shaved pecorino through the shredded sprouts, then taste and adjust the seasoning, if needed.

3 SPROUT & POTATO CAKES

Swap 350g Brussels sprouts, trimmed and shredded, for the savoy cabbage in my Colcannon Patties (page 178). Continue the recipe as written, serving them as per the recipe with curry mayo, or with a spoonful of cranberry sauce. A wonderful festive breakfast.

4 GNOCCHI & SPROUT GRATIN

Trim and halve 350g sprouts, tossing them with olive oil, salt and black pepper. Pour out onto a baking tray and roast at 160°C fan/350°F/gas 4 for 20–30 minutes, stirring halfway through, until tender in the middle and golden at the edges. Meanwhile, make the cheese sauce as per the Cauliflower Gnocchi Cheese (page 259). Stir the roasted sprouts and 500g fresh gnocchi through the cheese sauce and transfer into a baking dish. Make a quick crumb with 60g stale bread, 25g pecans and a handful of sage leaves in a food processor, sprinkle it over the gratin and bake for 20–25 minutes, or until golden and bubbling.

5 STIR-FRIED

Gently fry 1 finely sliced red onion in a good glug of olive oil and a pinch of salt and black pepper until soft and translucent. Add 2 tbsp balsamic glaze, continuing to fry until the onion is sticky and caramelized. In another pan, stir-fry 500g trimmed and shredded Brussels sprouts and a pinch of salt and black pepper over a medium-high heat for 5 minutes or so, until slightly charred. Stir through the caramelized onion and a knob of butter and serve finished with another crack of black pepper.

6 BRUSSELS SPROUT KINDA CAESAR SALAD

Combine the juice of 1 lemon, 1 tsp Dijon mustard, 2 tbsp tahini, 2 tbsp extra virgin olive oil, 1 minced garlic clove and a small handful of chopped capers in a jug. Thin it out with water, until it is a pourable consistency, then season to taste. Combine the dressing, 650g trimmed and shredded Brussels sprouts, 2 handfuls of chunky croutons, a handful of Parmesan shavings and 2 sliced spring onions in a mixing bowl. Mix well to combine, then taste and adjust the seasoning, if needed.

7 QUICK, CREAMY SPROUT PASTA

Cook 200g pasta according to the packet instructions. Meanwhile, fry 200g of trimmed and shredded sprouts with 2 cloves of finely sliced garlic for 5 minutes or so, until the sprouts have softened and are turning golden. Add the zest of 1 lemon, 100g ricotta, a good dash of the pasta cooking water and a pinch of salt and black pepper and mix to form a sauce. Stir through the cooked pasta and the juice of ½ lemon, then taste and adjust the seasoning, adding a dash of extra pasta water to loosen the sauce, if needed. Serve with plenty of grated Parmesan.

8 SPROUTS & CHESTNUTS

Fry 200g cooked roughly chopped chestnuts in a glug of olive oil over a high heat, until darkening at the edges. Tip out of the pan and add a glug more olive oil. Add 1kg trimmed whole Brussels sprouts, salt, black pepper and a glug of water, clamp on the lid and cook for 5 minutes or so, until tender all the way through. Remove the lid, add a generous knob of butter and fry for a further few minutes, until the Brussels sprouts have some colour. Stir through the chestnuts and taste and adjust the seasoning, if needed.

9 BRUSSELS SPROUT PAKORAS

Combine 200g gram flour, 25g plain flour, a small chunk of grated ginger, a handful of fresh coriander, ½ tsp turmeric, 1 tsp ground cumin, 1 tsp ground coriander, 1 tsp fenugreek and a good pinch of salt and black pepper in a mixing bowl. Add 225ml cold sparkling water and whisk into a smooth batter. Stir through ½ sliced chilli, 200g trimmed and shredded Brussels sprouts and 1 small finely sliced onion. Heat roughly 7cm of neutral oil in a medium pan over a medium heat. Once hot, deep-fry tablespoons of the batter until crisp on the outside and cooked all the way through, then serve with a mint chutney, or maybe a raita.

10 GRUYÈRE & CREAM SPROUTS

Trim and roughly shred 450g Brussels sprouts, then steam until al dente. Meanwhile, fry 1 finely chopped shallot and 2 sliced garlic cloves in a good knob of butter, until soft and translucent. Add 250ml double cream, a grating of nutmeg, salt and black pepper and bring to a gentle simmer. Cook for 5 minutes or so, until the cream has reduced and easily coats the back of a spoon. Add the steamed Brussels sprouts and 50g grated Gruyère and stir to melt the cheese. Taste and adjust the seasoning, if needed.

Shredded Sprout & Golden Lemon Salad

Every food writer will have a handful of recipes that readers seem to gravitate towards the most. This is one of mine. It's a pleasant surprise, as there are still plenty of sprout haters out there, but I hope that this recipe has converted some of them.

Shredding and roasting the sprouts creates a variety of textures – some bits crispy, some bits soft and silky. The golden lemon dressing is inspired by the cookery writer Carolina Gelen. It is a revelation! Use the whole lemon, pith and all, and fry until soft, golden and caramelized.

(See photo on previous page.)

Preheat the oven to 200°C fan/425°F/gas 7.

Combine the sliced Brussels sprouts, a good glug of olive oil and a nice pinch of salt in a mixing bowl. Use your hands to give everything a mix, then pour out onto a large baking tray and roast for 20–25 minutes, stirring halfway through, until the sprouts are turning golden and crisp.

Meanwhile, roughly dry the chickpeas with a tea towel. Combine with a glug of olive oil, a good pinch of salt and ½ tsp black pepper in a mixing bowl. Give everything a good stir, then pour out onto another baking tray. Roast alongside the Brussels sprouts for 20–25 minutes, giving them a shake halfway through, until golden brown and crunchy.

To make the dressing, heat a large frying pan over a medium heat and add a good glug of extra virgin olive oil. Once hot, add the lemon slices and cook for 2–3 minutes each side, until amber in colour and beginning to caramelize (the lemons tend to caramelize at different times, so just remove each one from the pan when they look ready – you don't want them to burn, as it will make the dressing bitter). Transfer the lemon slices to a small food processor, along with any oil left from the pan, and combine with the maple syrup, garlic, mustard, 2 tablespoons extra virgin olive oil and a good pinch of salt and pepper. Blitz into a rough paste (it won't be pourable like a regular dressing, but this is what you want), then taste and adjust the seasoning, if needed. If you don't have a small food processor, or a smaller bowl on a regular food processor, chop the golden lemons very finely and whisk with the remaining dressing ingredients.

SERVES 2

650g Brussels sprouts, trimmed and thinly sliced
olive oil
400g tin chickpeas, drained and rinsed
25g panko breadcrumbs
15g pine nuts
salt and freshly ground black pepper

DRESSING
extra virgin olive oil
1 unwaxed lemon, thinly sliced
1 tbsp maple syrup
1 garlic clove, minced
1 tsp wholegrain mustard

Finally, combine the panko breadcrumbs and pine nuts in a dry frying pan over a low-medium heat. Stir until golden and toasted, then remove from the heat.

Toss the roasted sprouts, half the roasted chickpeas and a good spoonful of the dressing in a mixing bowl. Taste and stir through another spoonful of dressing at a time, until you are happy (I normally end up using all the dressing, but any leftovers will keep for a few days in the fridge). Serve between bowls and finish with a sprinkling of the remaining chickpeas, and the golden breadcrumbs and pine nuts.

Curried Parsnips, Mango Halloumi

Here is something a little different to eat in the winter. A root vegetable salad is a welcome departure from more traditional winter weather fare. The parsnips are roasted until golden and tender, warm and earthy with spices. The halloumi is sticky and sweet with mango chutney. Both are united with a drizzle of melted butter, rich in garlic and curry leaf. It's exciting – some spice to chase away the chill.

Use fresh curry leaves if you can find them. If you can't, dried are fine too.

Preheat the oven to 200°C fan/425°F/gas 7.

Bring a large pan of salted water to the boil. Add the parsnips and bring the water back to a boil. Cook for 12–15 minutes, or until the parsnips can be easily pierced with a fork, but are keeping their shape. Drain and allow to steam dry.

Combine the par-cooked parsnips, chickpeas, cumin seeds, curry powder, a really generous glug of neutral oil and a nice pinch of salt and black pepper in a mixing bowl. Use your hands to give everything a good mix, then pour out between two baking trays. Roast for 35–45 minutes, stirring everything halfway through, until the parsnips are golden and the chickpeas are crispy.

Meanwhile, combine the yoghurt, lime juice and a pinch of salt in a small bowl. Taste and adjust the seasoning, if needed.

Ten minutes before the parsnips are due out of the oven, melt the butter in a small pan over a medium heat. Let it bubble for a minute or so, until it has slightly darkened in colour. Add the curry leaves and garlic, then remove the pan from the heat, letting the garlic soften in the residual heat.

Finally, make your mango halloumi. Heat a glug of neutral oil in a large frying pan over a medium heat. Once hot, fry the halloumi for 2–3 minutes each side, until lightly golden. Stir through the mango chutney and nigella seeds and continue to fry for a further minute or so, or until the halloumi is sticky and darkening at the edges.

Arrange the parsnips and chickpeas on a serving plate. Dollop over the yoghurt and drizzle with the curry leaf butter. Scatter with the halloumi and coriander, and finish with a good crack of black pepper. Eat it on its own, or with fluffy naans, if you like.

SERVES 4

- 1kg parsnips, peeled and chopped into thick batons
- 700g jar chickpeas (large chickpeas are best), drained and rinsed
- 1 tsp cumin seeds
- 1 tbsp mild curry powder
- neutral oil
- 100g thick plain yoghurt
- juice of ½ lime
- 25g salted butter
- 12 curry leaves
- 2 garlic cloves, finely sliced
- 400g halloumi, cubed
- 2 tbsp mango chutney
- 1 tsp nigella seeds
- handful of fresh coriander, leaves picked
- salt and freshly ground black pepper
- naan bread, if you like, to serve

Burnt Leeks & Cannellini Beans

I think my love affair with beans may become obvious as you look through this book – they make a perfect base for so many dishes. It pleases me that we're seeing some top-quality bean brands popping up in the UK now. I'm not a fanatic about many things, but I do think you should buy the beans in the glass jars because they are vastly, indisputably better than the ones in tins. You can cook your own if you like, but quite honestly, I can't be bothered.

Burning leeks is an interesting technique. The skin blackens on the outside, leaving a buttery-soft centre. I am often asked how to clean leeks when cooking them whole. Wash them thoroughly under running water, flaring the leaves and using the pressure of the water to force the dirt out. You won't get it all, but you'll be discarding the outside few layers here anyway, so you'll be okay.

~~~~~~~~~~~~~~~~~~

Preheat the oven to 200°C fan /425°F/gas 7.

Trim the top off the leeks at the point in which they start to flare. Place in a baking dish and roast for 35–40 minutes, or until the outside of each leek has blackened and burnt.

Heat 2 tablespoons of olive oil in a medium-sized ovenproof pan set over a medium heat (I always think a cast iron pan is nice here). Once hot, add the flour and garlic and whisk vigorously to form a paste; continue to whisk for a minute or so, to cook off the flour.

Next, combine the milk and white wine in a large jug. Pour a little of the liquid into the pan and whisk energetically until completely smooth. Then repeat this step, adding small amounts of the liquid and whisking until smooth, until you have a silky, creamy sauce. Add the rosemary sprig, bring the sauce to a gentle simmer and cook, whisking frequently, for 5–6 minutes, until thickened and glossy. Stir through the Parmesan, then season to taste with salt and black pepper.

Chop each blackened leek in half lengthways and use a spoon to scoop out the soft flesh in the middle, discarding the burnt skin. Give it a rough chop, then add it to the sauce, along with the cannellini beans. Stir well to combine, then transfer the whole pan into the oven and bake for 15–20 minutes, until gorgeously golden and bubbling out of the dish. Serve with lots of good crusty bread, to scoop and dip.

SERVES 4

- 4 large leeks
- olive oil
- 2 tbsp plain flour
- 4 large garlic cloves, grated
- 300ml milk
- 100ml dry white wine
- 1 sprig of rosemary
- 40g Parmesan, grated
- 700g jar cannellini beans, drained and rinsed
- salt and freshly ground black pepper
- crusty bread, to serve

Griddled Za'atar Cauliflower & Tofu Cream

SERVES 2, AS A MAIN WITH FLATBREADS

extra virgin olive oil
1 cauliflower, chopped into smallish florets and stalk chopped into chunks
large handful of mint, leaves picked and finely chopped
handful of basil, finely chopped
1 tbsp za'atar
1 garlic clove, grated
salt and freshly ground black pepper

TOFU CREAM
200g extra firm tofu
1 tbsp nutritional yeast
1 tbsp tahini
juice of 1 lemon

TO SERVE
roasted shelled pistachios, roughly chopped
a little grated lemon zest
flatbreads

Cauliflower is having a bit of a moment. It has leapt out of its classic cauliflower cheese coat and is hanging around on plates all over the place. I like it best griddled until marked with smoky lines, but retaining a little bite. It would be quite easy for me to gobble this whole plate down for lunch, mopping up the sauce up with a flatbread, but it is enough for two. It works as a side dish too, or as part of a larger spread. Just don't throw the cauli greens away – you can save them and roast them. If you don't have any nutritional yeast for the tofu cream, swap it for 1 teaspoon of white miso paste.

Start by making the tofu cream. Combine the tofu, nutritional yeast, tahini, lemon juice, 1 tablespoon of water and a pinch of salt in a high-powered blender. Blitz until creamy and completely smooth (you might need an extra dash of water to help your blender along here. Try not to add too much more liquid though, as it will make the tofu cream too runny), then taste and adjust the seasoning, if needed.

Heat a good glug of extra virgin olive oil in a griddle pan over a medium heat. Once hot, griddle the cauliflower florets and a good pinch of salt for 5–6 minutes each side, until darkly golden and charred with griddle marks.

Combine the warm griddled cauliflower with the mint, basil, za'atar, garlic, a good glug of extra virgin olive oil and a pinch of salt in a mixing bowl. Give everything a stir to combine, then taste and adjust the seasoning, if needed.

Spread the tofu cream over the base of a serving plate. Spoon the cauliflower on top and drizzle with any oil still left in the bowl. Finish with a few chopped roasted pistachios, a grating of lemon zest and a good grind of black pepper. Serve with soft, warm flatbreads.

Leek, Thyme & Butter Bean Gratin

This is a marriage of tender leeks and hearty beans brought together with a velvety sauce, a little thyme, a touch of mustard and a golden bubbling crust. The edges crisp and caramelize as the gratin bakes, transforming the simple into the sublime – it's a dish that feels as much like an embrace as it does a meal.

I will happily eat this on its own, but my Zesty Kale Salad (page 222) is always welcome on the side. For maximum indulgence, it also makes a delicious side dish alongside a roast dinner.

Preheat the oven to 200°C fan/425°F/gas 7.

Heat a good glug of olive oil in a medium ovenproof frying pan set over a medium heat. Once hot, fry the sliced leeks and a good pinch of salt in two batches, for 3–4 minutes on each side, until the edges are turning a dark golden (add a dash more oil between batches, if needed). Remove from the pan and set aside.

Wipe out the pan, then add the butter and melt over a medium heat. Add the flour and whisk vigorously to form a paste; continue to whisk for a minute or so, to cook off the flour.

Next, combine the milk and vegetable stock in a large jug. Pour a little of the liquid into the pan and whisk energetically until completely smooth. Then repeat this step, adding small amounts of the liquid and whisking until smooth, until you have a silky, creamy sauce. Bring the sauce to a gentle simmer and cook, whisking frequently, for 6–8 minutes, until thickened and glossy (we are looking for a sauce with the consistency of double cream). Stir through the miso paste and mustard, then season to taste with salt and black pepper. Remove from the heat.

Meanwhile, combine the stale bread, hazelnuts, thyme, lemon zest, and a good pinch of salt and black pepper in a food processor. Blitz into a chunky breadcrumb consistency.

Stir both the caramelized leeks and butter beans into the sauce. Sprinkle over the breadcrumb mixture and pat it down into an even layer. Transfer the whole pan to the oven and bake for 18–22 minutes, or until golden on top and bubbling through at the edges.

Finish with a extra crack of black pepper before serving.

SERVES 3–4

- olive oil
- 3 large leeks, cleaned and chopped into 2cm slices
- 50g unsalted butter
- 3 tbsp plain flour
- 300ml milk
- 400ml vegetable stock
- 1 tbsp white miso paste
- 2 tsp wholegrain mustard
- 85g stale bread (about 2 slices), torn into chunks
- 50g blanched hazelnuts
- 6 sprigs of thyme, leaves picked
- zest of 1 lemon
- 700g jar butter beans, drained and rinsed
- salt and freshly ground black pepper

Creamy Leek Tart

During the winter months, various friends and I gather every Sunday for a roast dinner. People drop in and out of The Roast Dinner Club each week, but when I can make it, I always suggest we have it at my house. I'm sure my friends think I'm just being kind, but really, my motive is to control the menu. A roast dinner must have parsnips. It must have red cabbage. And, it must have creamy leeks.

This tart is my way of eating creamy, cheesy leeks on the regular. Whether or not it's Sunday. Serve it either warm with mashed potatoes, or cold with a fresh vibrant salad. Whatever you fancy.

The leeks are cooked using a technique called 'butter poaching'. I first read about it in *The Secret Of Cooking* by Bee Wilson, who learnt it from Raymond Blanc in his 2011 book *Kitchen Secrets*. As he puts it, it's a 'great little secret for cooking vegetables; one that has served me well for many years'. It's the simplest, quickest way you can cook most vegetables, so it is worth remembering. You combine the prepared veg with a little water, a little butter and a pinch of salt in a saucepan. Clamp on the lid and cook it over the highest heat on the stove until the vegetables are tender and the butter has formed a silky emulsion. Carrots will take about 5 minutes, green beans about 3 minutes. Play around and see how you get on.

~~~~~~~~~~~~~~~~~

Start by making the pastry. Combine the flour and a pinch of salt in a mixing bowl. Add the butter and use your fingers to work it into the flour mixture, until you have something which resembles rough breadcrumbs. Add 1–2 tablespoons of ice-cold water and knead it together very briefly (careful not to overwork it) until the mixture forms a dough. Gently mould into a disc shape, wrap in clingfilm and refrigerate while you continue with the recipe. You can also do this in a food processor if you like; it's my preferred method. Pulse together the flour and salt, then add the butter and blitz until the mix resembles fine breadcrumbs. Blend as you add the water slowly through the tube in the top, until the dough balls up inside the processor bowl.

CUTS INTO 6

250g silken tofu
150g extra mature Cheddar, grated
50ml milk
1 tsp English mustard
½ tsp white pepper
1 tsp cornflour
2 leeks (or 3, if really small), chopped into even slices just shorter than the height of your tart tin
20g unsalted butter
salt

PASTRY
200g plain flour
100g unsalted butter, chilled and cubed
1–2 tbsp ice-cold water

Shape the dough into a disc, wrap and refrigerate. Preheat the oven to 170°C fan/375°F/gas 5.

On a floured surface, roll out your chilled dough into a circle the thickness of a £1 coin. Use it to line your tart tin (mine is 23cm in diameter, but slightly smaller is fine), pushing the pastry right into the sides and leaving an overhang at the top. Prick the bottom all over with a fork, then lay a sheet of parchment paper over the top and fill the case with baking beans (or dry lentils/rice). Blind bake for 15 minutes, then remove the beans and parchment paper and bake for a further 5–6 minutes, or until the base of the pastry case is lightly golden. Use a serrated knife to trim off any pastry overhang and nibble these bits while you continue with the recipe.

Combine the silken tofu, 125g of the Cheddar, milk, English mustard, white pepper, cornflour and a pinch of salt in a food processor. Blitz until smooth and creamy, then taste and adjust the seasoning, if needed.

Combine the leeks, butter, 50ml of water and a good pinch of salt in a smallish saucepan. Put the pan, with the lid on, over the highest heat on the stove and cook for 8 minutes, giving the pan an occasional shake, until the leeks are tender, but still keeping their shape. Remove from the heat, lift the lid and allow to steam dry.

Pour the sauce into the bottom of the pastry case and smooth it out. Press the slices of leek, cut sides up, into the sauce, then sprinkle over the remaining cheese. Bake for 30–35 minutes, or until the filling is a rich golden brown. Allow to cool for 20 minutes before cutting into slices and serving. It's good warm or cold.

Miso Onions & Puy Lentils

While I've been writing this book, my partner James hasn't had much of a chance to cook; something he loves doing. On one of the rare nights that we didn't have leftovers in the fridge, and I didn't have a recipe to test, he cooked this for me. It was pulled together from a few odds and ends in the cupboards – onions, pre-cooked bags of lentils, a scrap of cheese – and turned out to be the best meal he has ever made me. It's comforting and reassuring; like being wrapped in a hug. Together we've tweaked and refined it since, but this recipe remains an ode to that night. And to him, the love of my life.

SERVES 2, WITH LEFTOVERS

50g unsalted butter
3 onions, finely sliced
1½ tbsp brown sugar
6 sprigs of thyme, leaves picked
2 generous tbsp miso paste
2 tbsp boiling water
275ml vegetable stock
500g cooked Puy lentils (either from a packet or cooked in advance yourself)
70g extra mature Cheddar, grated
50g Parmesan, grated
salt and freshly ground black pepper

Heat a large heavy-bottomed ovenproof pan over a low-medium heat and add the butter. Once melted, add the sliced onion and a good pinch of salt and cook gently for 20–25 minutes, stirring regularly and reducing the heat if anything begins to catch, until the onion is soft and beginning to caramelize. Add the sugar and thyme and continue to cook for a further 3–5 minutes, or until the onion is lovely and sticky.

Preheat the oven to 200°C fan/425°F/gas 7.

Combine the miso paste with 2 tablespoons of just-boiled water and stir until smooth. Add it to the pan along with the vegetable stock and cooked Puy lentils. Stir well, then increase the heat slightly and bring everything to a boil. Simmer for a minute or so, stirring frequently, then remove from the heat. The miso should have seasoned the dish well enough here, but give it a taste and add a touch more salt, if you think it needs it.

Sprinkle both the grated cheeses over the top of the oniony lentils. Finish with a good crack of black pepper, then bake for 15–20 minutes, or until the cheese is golden and the lentils are bubbling between the cracks. Eat it on its own, or with a punchy lemony kale salad on the side. The combination is wonderful.

A Very Special Lasagne

This is another idea for those bobbly little Jerusalem artichokes – they make this lasagne a very special one. A gently cheesy sauce, a crunch of walnuts and a very healthy dose of artichokes. It's both hearty and refined.

The lumps and bumps on the artichokes make them a little fiddly to peel. I'll always rope someone in to help me, chatting as we work.

~~~~~~~~~~~~~~~~~~

Combine the milk, onion, bay leaves, thyme and peppercorns in your largest saucepan and bring to a boil over a medium heat. It will boil over if left for too long, so just watch it carefully here. Remove the pan from the heat and let the milk cool and infuse for an hour. Strain into a large jug (or two), discarding the herbs and peppercorns, but keeping the onion.

Meanwhile, heat a good glug of olive oil in your largest frying pan. Once hot, add the Jerusalem artichoke and a pinch of salt and fry for 10–12 minutes, stirring regularly, until it has softened and is a little golden. Add the kale and fry for a further few minutes, until wilted. Stir through the lemon juice, then remove the pan from the heat and set aside.

Preheat the oven to 160°C fan/350°F/gas 4.

Next, melt the butter in a large pan over a medium heat. I wash out my saucepan in which I infused the milk and use it here. Add the flour and whisk vigorously to form a rough paste; continue to whisk for a minute or so, to cook off the flour. Pour a little of the infused milk into the pan and whisk energetically until completely smooth. Then repeat this step, adding small amounts of the infused milk and whisking until smooth, until you have a silky, creamy sauce. Bring the sauce to a gentle simmer and cook, whisking frequently, for 7–8 minutes, until thickened and glossy. Stir through the mozzarella, half of the Parmesan, the nutmeg, a pinch of salt and a few good grinds of black pepper, until the cheese has melted. Taste and adjust the seasoning, if needed.

Crush the walnuts in a pestle and mortar, until they resemble rough breadcrumbs, and stir them through the Jerusalem artichokes and kale.

Recipe continues overleaf

SERVES 6

2 litres milk
1 onion, peeled and quartered
2 bay leaves
5 sprigs of thyme
10 peppercorns
olive oil
1kg Jerusalem artichokes, peeled and chopped into small cubes
200g kale, hard stems removed, finely chopped
juice of ½ lemon
80g unsalted butter
120g plain flour
250g fresh mozzarella, grated
100g Parmesan, finely grated
½ tsp freshly grated nutmeg
100g walnuts
14–18 dried lasagne sheets
12 sage leaves
salt and freshly ground black pepper

Finely chop the reserved softened onion and stir it through the filling too. Taste and adjust the seasoning, if needed.

Spread a quarter of the white sauce in a large lasagne dish and top with a third of the vegetable-nut filling. Top with a layer of lasagne sheets, then another quarter of the white sauce and a third of the vegetable-nut filling. Add another layer of lasagne sheets, then a quarter more white sauce and the remaining vegetable-nut filling. Cover with a final layer of lasagne sheets and the remaining white sauce. Sprinkle over the remaining Parmesan and dot around the sage leaves.

Bake the lasagne for 50 minutes–1 hour, until the edges are crisp, the top is golden and bubbling and the pasta in the middle has cooked through. Let it sit for 10 minutes, before chopping into slices and serving with a fresh, zingy salad. I like my Zesty Kale Salad from page 222 here. It makes a very special dinner.

Caramelized Onion & Potato Galette

There is something so gorgeously rustic about galettes. They are my favourite form of shortcrust pastry and the easiest way to make a tart. This one has caramelized onions, really thinly sliced potatoes and mountains of cheese. Hearty, yet somehow chic, my recipe was inspired by the flavours of a cheese and onion pasty – the most underrated pasty flavour, in my opinion.

You really do need a mandoline for this one. The potato should be sliced so thinly you can see light through it. They are more than worth the investment and will save you a not-insignificant amount of time in everyday cooking. I use it to slice the onion in this recipe, and other recipes, too.

(See photo overleaf.)

SERVES 4–6

olive oil
2 onions, finely sliced
2 tsp brown sugar
3 sprigs of thyme, leaves picked
2 large floury potatoes (King Edward, Cosmos, Désirée, etc.), peeled and very thinly sliced
40g salted butter
75g extra mature Cheddar, grated
50g Parmesan, grated
salt and freshly ground black pepper

PASTRY

240g plain flour, plus extra for dusting
125g unsalted butter, chilled and cubed
40–60ml ice-cold water

Start by making the pastry. Combine the flour and a pinch of salt in a mixing bowl. Add the butter and use your fingers to work it into the flour mixture, until you have something which resembles rough breadcrumbs. Add 40–60ml of ice-cold water and knead it together very briefly (careful not to overwork it) until the mixture forms a dough. Gently mould into a disc shape, wrap in clingfilm and refrigerate while you continue with the recipe. You can also do this in a food processor if you like; it's my preferred method. Pulse together the flour and salt, then add the butter and blitz until the mix resembles fine breadcrumbs. Blend as you add the water slowly through the tube in the top, until the dough balls up inside the processor bowl. Shape into a disc, wrap and refrigerate.

Meanwhile, heat a large frying pan over a low–medium heat and add a good glug of olive oil. Once hot, add the sliced onion and a good pinch of salt and cook gently for 15–20 minutes, stirring regularly and lowering the heat if they begin to catch, until the onion is soft and beginning to caramelize. Add the sugar and thyme and continue to cook for a further 5 minutes, until the onion is lovely and sticky.

Combine the sliced potato and butter in a large microwave-safe bowl. Microwave on high for 6–8 minutes, stirring thoroughly every minute, until the potato has softened and is bendy, but still keeping its shape.

Add the softened onions and a good pinch of salt and black pepper to the softened potatoes. Stir well to combine.

Recipe continues overleaf

Preheat the oven to 180°C fan/390°F/gas 6.

Place a large sheet of baking parchment over your work surface and sprinkle with flour. Roll out the pastry with a floured rolling pin, on top of the baking parchment, into a large rough circle approximately 35cm in diameter (it will be too large for your baking tray at this point, but you'll be folding in the edges).

Arrange half of the potato-onion mixture in the centre of the pastry circle, leaving a 5cm border the whole way around. Sprinkle over half of the Cheddar and Parmesan, then pile up most of the remaining potato-onion mixture on top and sprinkle with the remaining cheese. Finish with the remaining few bits of the potato-onion mixture, then gently fold the excess pastry over the filling, using the baking parchment underneath to help lift it. Brush the visible pastry with a little olive oil and grind everything with black pepper.

Transfer the galette, still on the baking parchment, onto a baking tray (don't hesitate here; one quick swift drag onto the tray). Bake for 45–55 minutes, until the pastry is golden and the filling is bubbling. Allow to rest for 15 minutes before serving. It's delicious on its own, or with a lemony side salad.

Roasted Jerusalem Artichoke Risotto

Despite their name, Jerusalem artichokes aren't related to the globe artichoke and instead belong to the sunflower family (they are called 'sunchokes' in the US, which makes a little more sense). They are knobbly and unassuming on the outside, with a sweet, white, nutty flesh on the inside. For me, they signal the year is coming to a close and that Christmas is on the horizon. A wonderful thing. If you are new to Jerusalem artichokes, this is a really lovely way to try them; I think it exhibits them in all their delicious glory.

Heat the oven to 180°C fan/390°F/gas 6.

Combine the chopped Jerusalem artichoke, a good glug of olive oil and a nice pinch of salt and black pepper on a baking tray. Use your hands to give everything a mix, then roast for 25–30 minutes, stirring once halfway through, until tender and golden.

Meanwhile, heat a glug of olive oil and 25g of the butter in a large heavy-bottomed pan set over a medium heat. Once hot, add the shallot, celery and a pinch of salt and fry for 6–8 minutes, stirring frequently, until soft and translucent.

Stir through the rice to coat it in the oil. Cook for a further 2 minutes, or until the rice turns a little translucent. Pour in the white wine and allow to simmer and bubble for a minute or so, until almost evaporated. Pour yourself a glass of wine too, and relax into the stirring.

Add a ladleful of the hot stock to the pan and stir continuously. Once all the liquid has been absorbed into the rice, add another ladleful of stock. Repeat this step, stirring continuously between ladlefuls of stock, until the rice is creamy but still slightly al dente (if you run out of stock, you can either make up a little more or just use boiling water). This should take you about 30 minutes; stick some music on.

Stir the Parmesan, remaining butter and most of the roasted Jerusalem artichoke through the risotto, until the butter has melted. Remove from the heat, then taste and adjust the seasoning, if needed.

Ladle the risotto generously between bowls and top with the remaining roasted Jerusalem artichoke, chopped toasted hazelnuts, a drizzle of truffle oil and a grating of lemon zest.

SERVES 4

- 300g Jerusalem artichokes, peeled and chopped into small cubes
- olive oil
- 75g unsalted butter
- 2 banana shallots, finely chopped
- 2 celery sticks, finely chopped
- 300g risotto rice (Carnaroli is my favourite)
- 175ml dry white wine
- 1–1.5 litres hot vegetable stock
- 25g Parmesan, grated
- salt and freshly ground black pepper

TO SERVE

- small handful of toasted hazelnuts, roughly chopped
- really good truffle oil
- a little grated lemon zest

Rice, Lentils, Crispy Onions

This is by no means a traditional mujadara (or majaddara), but it is my inspiration, nonetheless. A comforting Middle Eastern dish, mujadara is made of three main ingredients – rice, lentils, onion – but the recipe varies across the region. I've had the pleasure of eating plenty of Middle Eastern food when travelling in the region and it has held a place in my heart ever since.

This is a dish of simple ingredients, simple technique and simple flavour. Which sometimes, is exactly what you need. The crispy onions aren't always served with the dish, but I think they're essential.

Bring a pan of salted water to the boil. Add the brown lentils, cover the pan with a lid and cook for 12 minutes (this won't cook them through, we are just parboiling them at this point). Drain, then set aside.

Meanwhile, heat a large frying pan over a low–medium heat and add a good glug of olive oil. Once hot, add the sliced onions and a good pinch of salt and cook gently for 20–25 minutes, stirring regularly and lowering the heat if it starts to catch, until the onion is soft and turning golden. Add the brown sugar and cumin seeds and continue to cook for a further 5 minutes, or until the onion is sticky and golden brown.

Stir the rice, par-cooked lentils and a really good pinch of salt through the onions. Pour in the vegetable stock, stir well and bring to a boil. Reduce the heat to low, cover the pan with a lid and cook undisturbed for 15–20 minutes, or until the water has been absorbed fully (when you open the lid to check, you'll find that the grains of rice sat at the top of the pan look a little undercooked, but they will soften in the resting time). Remove from the heat and allow to sit, still covered, for 10 minutes.

Meanwhile, make the crispy onions. Combine the onion rounds, cornflour, ground cumin and a pinch of salt in a mixing bowl and stir well to coat. Heat roughly 5cm of neutral oil in a medium pan set over a medium heat. Once hot, fry the onion in two batches, until golden and crispy. Use a slotted spoon to remove them from the oil and onto a few sheets of kitchen towel, to soak up any excess grease.

Serve the rice with the crispy onions on top and with bowls of labneh/Greek yoghurt, fresh parsley and a pinch pot of black pepper on the table, for everyone to serve themselves.

SERVES 4

- 200g dried brown lentils, rinsed
- olive oil
- 2 large onions, finely sliced
- 2 tsp brown sugar
- 1 tsp cumin seeds
- 200g long-grain rice (not the easy-cook variety)
- 575ml vegetable stock
- salt and freshly ground black pepper

TO SERVE

- labneh or thick Greek yoghurt
- handful of parsley, leaves picked

CRISPY ONIONS

- 1 onion, sliced into very fine rounds
- 2 tbsp cornflour
- 2 tsp ground cumin
- neutral oil

A Very Wintery Pasta

Once a year, my mum would buy me a bag of hot roasted chestnuts from the stall in our town centre. Looking back, I think they were a pacifier. I would slowly unsheath each one from its armour as my mum frantically completed her Christmas shopping. I loved the way they warmed my hands, like a bite-sized hot water bottle in my pocket. I'll still buy a paper bag full of roasted chestnuts every time I see a stall. Not as a pacifier now, but as a nostalgic treat.

I'll have an open fire one day, but until then, I roast my chestnuts in the oven like we are doing here. If you do have a fire, cut a deep X into each chestnut, place in a cast-iron pan and cook on the embers for 10–12 minutes, until the shell splits open. Bliss!

If you don't want the bother, you could also use pre-cooked shelled chestnuts – 225g will do the job.

SERVES 6

1 small celeriac, peeled and chopped into small cubes
4 sprigs of rosemary, leaves picked
olive oil
450g chestnuts (in their shells)
1 onion, finely chopped
4 garlic cloves, sliced
1 litre vegetable stock
3 tbsp white miso paste
550g pasta (any type you like; I use malfalde here)
24 sage leaves
salt and freshly ground black pepper
a little grated lemon zest, to serve

Preheat the oven to 200°C fan/425°F/gas 7.

Combine the celeriac, rosemary, a good pinch of salt and a few really nice cracks of black pepper on a baking tray. Drizzle with a good glug of olive oil, then use your hands to give everything a mix. Roast for 30–40 minutes, stirring once halfway through, until tender all the way through and turning golden at the edges.

Cut a deep X shape on both sides of each of your chestnuts. Place in a baking dish and roast alongside the celeriac for 15–20 minutes, until the shells start to pull back and expose the flesh inside. When cool enough to touch, peel off the shells and discard, keeping the flesh inside.

Heat a good glug of olive oil in a large frying pan over a medium heat. Once hot, add the onion and a pinch of salt and fry for 6–8 minutes, until soft and translucent. Add the garlic and fry for a further minute or so, just to soften.

Add the roasted celeriac, roasted chestnuts, vegetable stock and miso paste to the pan. Stir well and bring to a gentle simmer. Reduce the heat slightly, then cook for 5 minutes, stirring regularly, until the liquid has reduced slightly and the celeriac is uber soft. Remove from the heat.

Next, cook your pasta according to the packet instructions.

While the pasta is cooking, use a hand blender to blend the contents of the pan into a smooth and silky sauce (you can also do this in a stand blender, just let it cool down slightly first). It will be thick, but don't fret. Taste and adjust the seasoning, if needed.

Heat a really good glug of olive oil in a small frying pan over a medium–high heat. Once hot, add the sage leaves and fry for 20–30 seconds, until crisp. Use a slotted spoon to remove them from the oil and onto a sheet of kitchen towel, to soak up any excess grease.

Lift the pasta from its pan and into the sauce with a pair of tongs, bringing some of the pasta water along with it. Stir well to combine, adding a splash more pasta water to loosen everything up, if needed. Twist into bowls and finish with a few crispy sage leaves and a good crack of black pepper.

Cauliflower Gnocchi Cheese & a Green Crumb

The cauliflower, the chameleon vegetable. Delicious in many forms, but arguably most beloved when drenched in a glossy cheese sauce. I have no problem with a trayful of cauliflower cheese for dinner – in fact, I encourage it – but the gnocchi and verdant crumb make this dish feel slightly more dinner-appropriate. It's a great one for children too.

I certainly have room to improve when it comes to utilizing my freezer, but this dish is always one I'll double up on, freezing half in a baking dish to defrost and heat on another day. A spare cauliflower gnocchi cheese in the freezer? What a comforting thought.

~~~~~~~~~~~~~~~~~~

Preheat the oven to 180°C fan/350°F/gas 4.

Chop the cauliflower into florets and its leaves into thirds. Combine both on a large baking tray and drizzle with a good glug of olive oil and a pinch of salt and black pepper. Use your hands to give everything a mix, then roast for 20–25 minutes, giving everything a mix halfway, until the florets are soft all the way through and the leaves are getting crispy on the edges.

Meanwhile, melt the butter in a large ovenproof frying pan over a medium heat. Add the garlic and a pinch of salt and fry for a minute or so, just to soften. Add the English mustard powder and flour and whisk vigorously to form a paste. Continue to whisk for a minute or so, to cook off the flour.

Next, combine the milk and vegetable stock in a large jug. Pour a little of the liquid into the pan and whisk energetically until completely smooth. Then repeat this step, adding small amounts of the liquid and whisking until smooth, until you have a silky, creamy sauce. Bring the sauce to a gentle simmer, then reduce the heat to low and cook for 8–10 minutes, whisking frequently, until thickened and glossy (we are looking for the consistency of thick double cream). Stir through the grated cheese, then season to taste with salt and black pepper.

Meanwhile, combine the stale bread, hazelnuts, capers, parsley and a good pinch of salt and black pepper in a food processor. Blitz into chunky breadcrumb consistency.

Add the roasted cauliflower and fresh gnocchi to the sauce. Stir well to combine, then scatter over the green crumb. Bake for 20–25 minutes, or until the top has darkened and the sauce around the edge is bubbling. Serve with a fresh zesty salad. My Zesty Kale Salad on page 222 does the job perfectly.

SERVES 4

1 large cauliflower
olive oil
100g unsalted butter
2 garlic cloves, minced
2 tsp English mustard powder
85g plain flour
800ml milk
200ml vegetable stock
125g Cheddar, grated
60g stale bread
25g hazelnuts
2 tbsp capers, brine drained
small handful of parsley, stalks and all
500g fresh gnocchi
salt and freshly ground black pepper

Honey Teriyaki, Black Sesame & Sprout Udon

Perhaps once the most polarizing of vegetables, the humble Brussels sprout is having a renaissance and I'm so pleased about it. I like this way of eating them; like cabbage, they are lovely to stir-fry. Their slight bitterness needs balancing, so they benefit from a sweet sauce like the honey teriyaki here. It's quick and perfect for a midweek meal. Add a protein too if you like – firm tofu, chicken, steak or whatever you wish.

Begin by making the sauce. Heat your smallest pan over a low-medium heat and add the honey, sugar, rice vinegar, soy sauce, ginger and garlic. Stir well to combine, then let it bubble and simmer for 2–3 minutes, until sticky and thickened. Remove the pan from the heat and stir through the butter and black sesame seeds, until the butter has melted. Set to one side while you continue with the recipe.

Next, heat a good glug of sesame oil in a large frying pan over a medium heat. Once hot, add the shredded Brussels sprouts and a pinch of salt and fry, stirring frequently, for 6–8 minutes, until the sprouts are bright green and starting to char on the edges.

Meanwhile, cook your noodles according to the packet instructions. Drain, reserving the cooking water.

Add both the noodles and the sauce to the pan with the Brussels sprouts and toss to coat, adding a dash or two of cooking water if you need to loosen the sauce. They should be gorgeous and glossy. If your sauce is too sticky to get it all out of the pan, add a dash of boiling water to it and warm it back up over a medium heat, until it has loosened. Taste and adjust the seasoning, adding a pinch of salt, if you think it needs it.

Serve between bowls, or eat them straight from the pan. They need no garnish, they're perfect as they are.

SERVES 2

3 tbsp runny honey
1 tbsp light brown soft sugar
1½ tbsp rice vinegar
2½ tbsp soy sauce
½ thumb-sized piece of ginger, grated
1 small garlic clove, grated
40g unsalted butter
1 tbsp black sesame seeds
sesame oil
200g Brussels sprouts, trimmed and shredded
300g udon noodles
salt

Winter Hummus Bowls

SERVES 2, WITH LEFTOVERS

1 cauliflower, chopped into florets and leaves roughly chopped
3 tbsp harissa
2 tsp ground cumin
olive oil
150g cooked Puy lentils
juice of ½ lemon
small handful of parsley, leaves picked and finely chopped
1 tsp sumac
vegetable oil, for frying
1 small onion, very finely sliced
2 tbsp cornflour
salt and freshly ground black pepper

HERBY HUMMUS
400g tin chickpeas, drained and rinsed
1 garlic clove, peeled
small handful of dill, leaves picked
handful of parsley leaves
1 heaped tbsp tahini
½ tsp cumin
juice of ½ lemon
extra virgin olive oil

TO SERVE
pomegranate seeds
flatbreads

There are many reasons I like this recipe, but one of them is that every component of this bowl can be pre-prepared. Meaning that if you do want to eat this as a quick lunch, it's just an assembly jobby. You can keep the base of this recipe the same and change the vegetables throughout the seasons: beetroot and potatoes in the autumn; fennel, aubergine and courgette in the summer; and Jersey Royals and purple sprouting broccoli in the spring.

Preheat the oven to 160°C fan/350°F/gas 4.

Combine the cauliflower and its leaves, harissa, cumin, a good glug of olive oil and a pinch of salt in a large bowl. Use your hands to give everything a good mix and rub the spices into the cauliflower, then tip out on a baking tray. Roast for 30–35 minutes, or until tender all the way through and starting to char on the edges.

Meanwhile, to make the herby hummus, combine the chickpeas, garlic, dill and parsley, tahini, cumin, lemon juice and a really good pinch of salt and black pepper in a food processor. Blitz the mixture, adding 4–5 tablespoons extra virgin olive oil in a thin stream through the hole in the top, until the hummus is smooth and creamy. Taste and adjust the seasoning, if needed.

To make the marinated lentils, combine the cooked Puy lentils, lemon juice, parsley, sumac and a pinch of salt and black pepper in a bowl. Stir well, then taste and adjust the seasoning, if needed.

Finally, make the crispy onions. Heat 2cm of vegetable oil in a small pan over a medium–high heat. Once hot, lightly dust the sliced onion in cornflour and fry in batches for a minute or so, until nice and crispy. Remove from the pan and spread onto kitchen roll, to remove any excess grease.

Spread a good dollop of hummus in the bottom of a serving bowl. Add a few spoonfuls of the marinated lentils on top, then the roasted cauliflower and a sprinkling of pomegranate seeds. Finish with the crispy onions and a good crack of black pepper. Serve with a warm flatbread on the side, to tear, dip and clean the bowl.

Blood Orange & Poppy Seed Loaf

Blood oranges, with their sweet, scarlet flesh, are at their best between January and March in the UK. Their season is short, so as soon as I can get my hands on them, I buy as many as I can and fill up my fruit bowl. Some years you'll find them less bloodied than usual, which is down to the weather in Sicily – the fiercer the winter, the sweeter and redder the oranges.

I call this a grown-up cake. The floral nuttiness of the poppy seeds makes an elegant pairing to the sharp zest of the blood orange. It's not too sweet either, which is just how I like it.

If you aren't planning on eating this cake on the same day, hold off from adding the blood orange slices until you are ready to serve – they don't keep so well.

CUTS INTO 10

125ml neutral oil
225ml milk
zest of 4 blood oranges
125ml blood orange juice (measure after zesting oranges)
1 tsp vanilla extract
pinch of salt
225g caster sugar
2 tbsp poppy seeds
300g self-raising flour
1 tsp baking powder

TO DECORATE
100g icing sugar
1–2 tbsp blood orange juice
slices of blood orange

Preheat the oven to 160°C fan/350°F/gas 4 and grease and/or line a loaf tin. Mine is 24cm in length, but one slightly shorter or longer is fine too.

Combine the oil, milk, blood orange zest and juice, vanilla extract and salt in a mixing bowl. Add the caster sugar and poppy seeds and whisk well to combine.

Sift both the self-raising flour and baking powder into the bowl and fold gently until fully combined. Pour the mixture into the prepared loaf tin and bake for 45–55 minutes, or until the top is cracked and golden, and a skewer inserted into the centre comes out clean. Let it sit for 15 minutes, before turning out onto a wire rack and allowing the cake to cool completely.

To make the icing, whisk together the icing sugar and blood orange juice until smooth, starting with less juice and adding more if needed, until thick but wet enough to drop off a spoon. Spoon over the cake and watch the icing run slowly over the sides. Finish with slices of fresh blood orange on top.

Pomegranate & Blood Orange Trifle

A dessert to celebrate the gorgeous winter fruits of the festive period. This is a very special pud.

Jelly or no jelly? It's a passionate subject. I'm all for the jelly, particularly this perfectly tart pomegranate jelly. But I realise the slightly soggy sponge isn't for everyone. To help with that, you could set the jelly in the bottom of the dish, then layer the sponge over the top.

You don't have to make your own custard or sponge here, so it is an easy dessert to pull together. You're serving a showstopper of a trifle, and, during the festive period with everything else there is to do, I think that's more than enough.

SERVES 8–10

710ml pomegranate juice
2 tbsp caster sugar
juice of ½ lemon
12g (2 sachets) vege-gel
400g Madeira loaf cake, thinly sliced
35ml Cointreau
4 blood oranges, peeled, sliced into rounds and seeds removed
750ml good-quality custard (I use the posh fresh custard in a tub), at room temperature
300g white chocolate, melted
500ml double cream
1 pomegranate, seeds only

TO SERVE

1 pomegranate, seeds only
small handful of chopped pistachios

Start by making the jelly. Combine the pomegranate juice, caster sugar, lemon juice and vege-gel in a saucepan. Place over a medium heat and stir constantly as you bring it to a boil. Once it reaches its boiling point, remove the pan from the heat and let it cool for 15 minutes.

Meanwhile, brush each slice of Madeira cake with a little Cointreau and push them into the base of a large glass serving dish – one that looks good for trifle. Any leftover Cointreau can just be poured over the sponges in their dish.

Place the orange slices around the edge of the dish, pushing them into the side of the glass and sitting the edge on top of the cake. Any that don't fit around the sides of the glass can lay on their sides on top of the cake. Ladle the jelly on top of the cake, letting it come up around the sides of the orange slices at the edge of the dish. Let the jelly set in the fridge. It should take 3–4 hours.

Once the jelly has set, combine the custard and melted white chocolate in a large bowl. Pour it over the jelly and smooth over the top. Return the dish to the fridge for a further hour (or longer if you're not serving it yet), to let the chocolate set.

Finally, when you are ready to serve, whip the cream to soft peaks. It's always best to under-whip rather than over-whip, so as soon as you think it's done, stop. Spread it roughly over the custard and sprinkle the pomegranate seeds and pistachios on top. Present the trifle smugly to the table and feel pleased with yourself as you gobble up your delicious creation.

Pear Fritters & Miso Caramel

I based these fritters on the warm sugared doughnuts I ate as a child, from the little huts on Brighton seafront. The smell of frying, the texture of their crumb; this recipe takes me back there.

Depending on the occasion, I serve these in one of two ways. For parties, I'll arrange them on a big platter, the ramekin of miso caramel on the side, passing them around for my friends to dip and enjoy. For dinners, I'll serve them in bowls, drizzling over the caramel, with a scoop of ice cream.

~~~~~~~~~~~~

Start with the miso caramel. Combine the caster sugar, butter and 1 tablespoon water in a medium saucepan. Place over a low–medium heat and stir for 2–3 minutes, until the sugar has dissolved and the mixture is combined. Increase the heat to medium and bring the pan to a boil. Boil the mixture for 4–5 minutes, stirring occasionally, until it's a rich amber colour. Watch it carefully here – it can turn from golden to burnt in a matter of seconds. Lower the heat, add the cream and miso paste and stir vigorously, until smooth and combined. It will splutter as you add the cream, so just be careful. Remove from the heat and set aside while you continue with the recipe.

Next, get the oil ready. Heat roughly 7cm of neutral oil in a medium pan over a medium heat. Let it heat up while you make the batter.

Combine the milk, eggs and melted butter in a mixing bowl and whisk until smooth. Sift in the flour, baking powder and cinnamon and add the sugar and salt. Gently fold the dry ingredients into the wet ingredients, until you have a thick, lump-free batter. Finally, stir through the pears and you are ready to cook.

Use two spoons to drop tablespoons of the mixture into the hot oil, piling it up on one spoon and using the other to scrape it off into the oil. Don't make them much bigger than this, or they won't cook in the middle. Fry 3 or 4 at a time, until they are deeply golden and crisp and floating to the top of the pan, gently ripping apart the first one to check the batter isn't still raw in the middle. They should take about 3–4 minutes each – if they are much quicker than this, you'll want to turn the heat down. Remove each one from the oil as it's ready and onto a few sheets of kitchen towel, to soak up any excess grease.

Warm the miso caramel back up over a medium heat, to thin out the sauce. Serve the fritters for you and your friends to dip and devour.

SERVES 6

neutral oil
125ml milk
2 medium eggs
125g unsalted butter, melted
250g plain flour
2 tsp baking powder
1 tsp ground cinnamon
100g caster sugar
pinch of salt
2 firm pears, peeled and chopped into 1cm cubes

MISO CARAMEL

200g caster sugar
50g unsalted butter
150ml double cream
2 tsp white miso paste

The Greyhound

I won the book *Born To Run* by Michael Morpurgo in a raffle when I was probably eight or nine years old. It centres around a greyhound called Bright Eyes, a dog who lives many different lives as he passes from owner to owner. The story fascinated me and as children do, I became hooked on the thought of owning a greyhound. Twenty years later, the idea still hadn't unstuck. I adopted my own ex-racing greyhound Poppy in 2023; the best decision I've made. It's a bit of a love story really.

I have to say, before Poppy, I hadn't given the greyhound cocktail much thought. However, I seem to be turning into a more clichéd 'dog mum' by the day, so it's now a regular drink of mine.

I should note that this cocktail isn't actually named after the hound, but after Greyhound bus stations where it was a signature cocktail.

This is how I like mine – not too sweet and with a good whack of rosemary.

MAKES 1

1 sprig of rosemary
25ml sugar syrup
50ml good quality vodka
150ml freshly-squeezed pink grapefruit juice

TO SERVE
slice of grapefruit
1 sprig of rosemary

Muddle the rosemary and sugar syrup together in a cocktail shaker, to release the rosemary's fragrance. Add the vodka, grapefruit juice and a handful of ice, then clamp on the lid and shake until the cocktail shaker has frosted on the outside.

Strain the cocktail into a rocks glass containing large ice cubes. Serve garnished with a slice of grapefruit and a fresh sprig of rosemary.

A MENU FOR EACH SEASON

I love hosting. I love creating menus, pairing dishes together, feeding my friends and family. Below are examples of menus I would put together for each season. But really, there are plenty of possibilities.

SPRING EARLY DINNER
For when the days are getting longer. The first time you can sit outside that year.

To drink: Rhubarb Sour (see page 72)

To start: A Very Quick Asparagus Tart (see page 22)

Main course: Spring Pea Risotto (see page 41)

Dessert: Ricotta Stove Cakes, Honey-poached Rhubarb (see page 67)

SUMMER LUNCH SPREAD
Plenty of friends and family. A sunny afternoon, in the garden, lots of chatting. The food on the table for everyone to help themselves to.

To drink: Frozen Peach Bellinis (see page 144)

To nibble: Blistered Broad Beans with Chilli, Lime & Salt (see page 81), Charred Corn, Avocado & Jalapeño Dip (see page 84), crisps

Main course: A Sabich Building Table (see page 134)

Dessert: Strawberry & Black Pepper Granita, Clotted Cream (see page 142)

AUTUMN DATE NIGHT
For you and your love. Candles lit, music playing.

To drink: Blackberry Old Fashioned (see page 208)

To start: Roasted Beetroot & Wasabi Soup (see page 170)

Main course: Miso Red Cabbage, Mash & Crispy Beans (see page 180)

Dessert: Ripe Figs, Honey Mascarpone, Pistachio Brittle (see page 202)

WINTER FESTIVE DINNER
Your favourite people all sat around one table. Twinkly lights and lots of silly games for after.

To drink: The Greyhound (see page 270)

To nibble: Chicory, Pears & Candied Thyme Walnuts (see page 219), Five Spice Kalettes & Peanut Dip (see page 218)

Main course: Miso, Onions & Puy Lentils (see page 246), Zesty Kale Salad (see page 222)

Dessert: Pomegranate & Blood Orange Trifle (see page 266)

A MENU FOR EACH SEASON

ABOUT GEORGIE

Food writer and cook Georgie Mullen started her career working in kitchens and as a recipe developer. She created her website and Instagram in 2018 to share her simple, seasonal recipes. Since then, she has taught technique and seasonality at her own cookery classes, has hosted supper clubs, and has built a huge online following. She lives in London. @georgieeats

ACKNOWLEDGEMENTS

This book would not have been possible without the many hands, hearts and kitchens that have contributed to it. I'm extraordinarily fortunate in owing so many people thanks.

First, to Lizzy Gray and Martha Burley, who have turned my Google Docs into something more beautiful than I could have imagined. Thank you for your skill, your sharp eye, and your steady belief that these recipes were worth sharing. And to the rest of the publishing team – Claire Rochford, Annie Lee, Sarah Prior, Sarah Badhan, Alexandra Watkins and Maya Conway. You've made writing my first book such a joy.

To Esther Clark and Matt Russell, thank you. You made my recipes come alive in a way I could never have hoped to do alone; a dream team. And to everyone who helped make our shoot days run so smoothly – Clare Cole, Caitlin Linnuala, Lauren Wall, Paola Sanchez, Evie Milsom, Claudia Gschwend, Rachel Ware, Tara Fisher.

To Clarisse, Alicia, Francesca, Minnie and the rest of the team at MVE – thank you for your unwavering support and belief in me; your guidance and steady presence have been invaluable in every step of this journey. You've created an environment that nurtures creativity and encourages growth, and I feel incredibly lucky to have you by my side.

To Oscar, my brilliant agent. You've guided me through the complex world of publishing with such grace and understanding. You've been both a sounding board and a guiding hand, and I am so thankful for everything you've done to bring this book to life.

To the friends who support me, encourage me and let me feed them – thank you. To Jess and Zak who have championed me from the very start; to Hannah, my confidant. And to Charlotte, Jose and Immie. You have all added to this collection of recipes, whether that be with a suggestion, or simply with your company whilst I chopped, stirred and tasted.

To my family – my dad, whose presence in my life is a source of constant reassurance. None of this would have been possible without your faith, love and support. To Pip, the person I turn to for clarity, whose advice is both wise and grounded. To Josie, Becky, Luke. My gorgeous family.

To James, the one who quietly holds everything together – thank you for being there, not just through the good days, but through the long hours, the late nights, the moments of uncertainty. You've been my rock, never wavering, always offering to help; you are the best washer-upper I know! Your patience and love are woven into every page of this book, and for that, I am forever grateful.

And finally, to you, the reader – thank you for picking up this book and welcoming it into your home. May it bring you many happy hours in the kitchen, sharing dinner with the people you love.

CONVERSION CHARTS

Weight

IMPERIAL	METRIC
¼ oz	10g
½ oz	15g
¾ oz	20g
1 oz	25g
1½ oz	40g
2 oz	50g
3 oz	75g
3½ oz	100g
4 oz	115g
4½ oz	125g
5 oz	150g
6 oz	175g
7 oz	200g
8 oz	225g
9 oz	250g
9½ oz	275g
10/11 oz	300g
12 oz	350g
13 oz	375g
14 oz	400g
15 oz	425g
16 oz (1 lb)	450g
1 lb 2 oz	500g (0.5kg)
1¼ lb	550g
1 lb 5 oz	600g
1½ lb	675g
1 lb 10 oz	725g
1¾ lb	800g
1 lb 14 oz	850g
2 lb	900g
2¼ lb	1kg

Volume

IMPERIAL	METRIC
1 fl oz (2 tbsp)	30ml
2 fl oz	50ml
3 fl oz	75ml
3½ fl oz	100ml
4 fl oz	125ml
5 fl oz (¼ pint)	150ml
6 fl oz	175ml
7 fl oz	200ml
8 fl oz	250ml
9 fl oz	275ml
10 fl oz (½ pint)	300ml
11 fl oz	325ml
12 fl oz	350ml
13 fl oz	375ml
14 fl oz	400ml
15 fl oz (¾ pint)	450ml
16 fl oz	475ml
18 fl oz	500ml
20 fl oz (1 pint)	600ml
1¼ pints (25 fl oz)	700ml
1½ pints (30 fl oz)	850ml
1¾ pints (35 fl oz)	1 litre

SPOONS (LIQUIDS)

1 tsp	5ml
1 tbsp (3 tsp)	15ml

RECIPE INDEX

MIDWEEK MEALS (UNDER 30 MINUTES)

152	A Blackberry Grilled Cheese
94	A Favourite Summer Salad
98	A Peach Panzanella Salad
22	A Very Quick Asparagus Tart
95	A Very Simple Tomato Salad
36	Beans al Limone with Asparagus & Peas
208	Blackberry Old Fashioned
81	Blistered Broad Beans with Chilli, Lime & Salt
231	Blood Orange & Radicchio Salad
215	Bruschetta with Maple Pears & Thyme Ricotta
90	Carrot & Poppy Seed Salad
84	Charred Corn, Avocado & Jalapeño Dip
32	Charred Peas, Mint, Chilli, Ricotta
219	Chicory, Pears & Candied Thyme Walnuts
91	Chilli Aioli & Thai Basil Corn
178	Colcannon Patties, Curry Mayo
124	Cold Peanut Noodles & Charred Lettuce
122	Creamed Corn Cannellini Beans
154	Golden Beetroot & Fig Salad
25	Griddled Asparagus & Caper Salsa Toast
171	Griddled Hispi Cabbage & Charred Jalapeño Sauce
241	Griddled Za'atar Cauliflower & Tofu Cream
260	Honey Teriyaki, Black Sesame & Sprout Udon
268	Pear Fritters & Miso Caramel
223	Persimmon, Burrata & Chilli Crisp
51	Purple Sprouting Broccoli & Tahini Beans
54	Purple Sprouting Broccoli Orecchiette & Chilli Pangrattato
117	Really Easy Tomato & Gnocchi Bake
67	Ricotta Stove Cakes, Honey-poached Rhubarb
202	Ripe Figs, Honey Mascarpone & Pistachio Brittle

100	Runner Bean Fattoush
133	Samphire & Brown Butter Bucatini
46	Silk Handkerchief Pasta with Wild Garlic Pesto *(if you don't make your own pasta)*
120	Spanakopita Beans
214	Sprout, Sticky Onion & Chestnut Toast
222	Zesty Kale Salad
121	Zhoug & Smoky Aubergine Sandwiches

SLOW WEEKEND COOKING

174	A Deep, Dark Cavolo Nero Curry
195	A Gorgeous Pumpkin Curry
134	A Sabich Building Table
130	A Very Herby Noodle Soup
249	A Very Special Lasagne
207	Apple & Ginger Tarte Tatin
105	Aubergine Schnitzel, Cucumber Salad
118	Aubergine Stew, Whipped Tahini Sauce
112	Aubergines & Golden Sauce
182	Baked Chard Conchiglioni
198	Beetroot Velvet Cake
263	Blood Orange & Poppy Seed Loaf
160	Butternut Squash & Barley Bowls, Halloumi Croutons
168	Butternut Squash & Black Rice Soup Bowls
251	Caramelized Onion & Potato Galette
228	Celeriac & Spelt Soup (with lots of crispy sage)
244	Creamy Leek Tart
172	Crimson Beetroot Dhal
128	Fennel & Sausage Pappardelle
140	Gooseberry Cake with Honey & Thyme Cream
37	Lemongrass, Coconut, Noodles, Greens
30	My Farinata with Asparagus & Peas
266	Pomegranate & Blood Orange Trifle
71	Rhubarb & Custard Blondies
201	Rice Pudding & Jammy Figs
249	Roasted Jerusalem Artichoke Risotto

53	Sausage, Borlotti & Spring Green Casserole
46	Silk Handkerchief Pasta with Wild Garlic Pesto *(when making your own pasta)*
127	Slow Cooked Courgette Tagliatelle
64	Soda Bread & Wild Garlic Butter
41	Spring Pea Risotto
142	Strawberry & Black Pepper Granita, Clotted Cream
184	Sweet Potato Gratin Pie
114	Tomato Curry, Crispy Tofu, Rice
227	Very Untraditional French Onion Soup
48	Wild Garlic Gnudi
188	Wild Mushroom Hotpot

PLANT-BASED

174	A Deep, Dark Cavolo Nero Curry (if making with tofu)
195	A Gorgeous Pumpkin Curry
95	A Very Simple Tomato Salad
256	A Very Wintery Pasta
118	Aubergine Stew, Whipped Tahini Sauce *(it using plant-based yoghurt)*
112	Aubergines & Golden Sauce
167	Autumn Pasta with Chickpeas (without Parmesan)
123	Bean Confit
157	Black Rice & Sweet Potato Salad
81	Blistered Broad Beans with Chilli, Lime & Salt
263	Blood Orange & Poppy Seed Loaf
168	Butternut Squash & Black Rice Soup Bowls
90	Carrot & Poppy Seed Salad
228	Celeriac & Spelt Soup (with lots of crispy sage)
91	Chilli Aioli & Thai Basil Corn
124	Cold Peanut Noodles & Charred Lettuce
172	Crimson Beetroot Dhal
226	Crispy Pan-fried Jerusalem Artichokes

109	Fennel, Tomato & Salsa Verde Traybake	32	Charred Peas, Mint, Chilli, Ricotta
218	Five Spice Kalettes & Peanut Dip	226	Crispy Pan-fried Jerusalem Artichokes
171	Griddled Hispi Cabbage & Charred Jalapeño Sauce	144	Frozen Peach Bellinis
		24	New Potato & Garlic Soup
241	Griddled Za'atar Cauliflower & Tofu Cream	223	Persimmon, Burrata & Chilli Crisp
		28	Purple Sprouting Broccoli Tempura & Lime Pickle Mayo
37	Lemongrass, Coconut, Noodles, Greens		
159	Lovely Autumn Veg & Grains with a Ginger Soy Dressing	79	Radish Butter
		82	Radishes Braised with Miso
246	Miso Onions & Puy Lentils	117	Really Easy Tomato & Gnocchi Bake
180	Miso Red Cabbage, Mash & Crispy Beans (if using non-dairy milk)	72	Rhubarb Sour
		47	Risi e Bisi
57	Parathas, Paneer, Pickled Rhubarb, Green Chutney	170	Roasted Beetroot & Wasabi Soup
		133	Samphire & Brown Butter Bucatini
51	Purple Sprouting Broccoli & Tahini Beans	46	Silk Handkerchiefs with Wild Garlic Pesto
117	Really Easy Tomato & Gnocchi Bake (without Parmesan)	151	Spicy Sweet Seeds
		150	Sticky Peanut Swede
47	Risi e Bisi	142	Strawberry & Black Pepper Granita, Clotted Cream
170	Roasted Beetroot & Wasabi Soup		
53	Sausage, Borlotti & Spring Green Casserole (if you use plant-based sausages)	270	The Greyhound
		43	Wild Garlic Pesto
		222	Zesty Kale Salad
236	Shredded Sprout & Golden Lemon Salad		
151	Spicy Sweet Seeds		
114	Tomato Curry, Crispy Tofu, Rice		
188	Wild Mushroom Hotpot		
262	Winter Hummus Bowls		
222	Zesty Kale Salad		
121	Zhoug & Smoky Aubergine Sandwiches		

6 INGREDIENTS OR LESS

152	A Blackberry Grilled Cheese
61	A Tartiflette for Spring
22	A Very Quick Asparagus Tart
80	Balsamic Strawberries & Stracciatella
123	Bean Confit
208	Blackberry Old Fashioned
81	Blistered Broad Beans with Chilli, Lime & Salt

DISHES TO PREPARE AHEAD

- 174 A Deep, Dark Cavolo Nero Curry
- 195 A Gorgeous Pumpkin Curry
- 134 A Sabich Building Table
- 130 A Very Herby Noodle Soup
- 95   A Very Simple Tomato Salad
- 249 A Very Special Lasagne
- 118 Aubergine Stew, Whipped Tahini Sauce
- 167 Autumn Pasta with Chickpeas
- 182 Baked Chard Conchiglioni
- 198 Beetroot Velvet Cake
- 157 Black Rice & Sweet Potato Salad
- 263 Blood Orange & Poppy Seed Loaf
- 240 Burnt Leeks & Cannellini Beans
- 160 Butternut Squash & Barley Bowls, Halloumi Croutons
- 168 Butternut Squash & Black Rice Soup Bowls
- 251 Caramelized Onion & Potato Galette
- 90   Carrot & Poppy Seed Salad
- 259 Cauliflower Gnocchi Cheese & a Green Crumb
- 228 Celeriac & Spelt Soup (with lots of crispy sage)
- 84   Charred Corn, Avocado & Jalapeño Dip
- 178 Colcannon Patties, Curry Mayo
- 244 Creamy Leek Tart
- 172 Crimson Beetroot Dhal
- 140 Gooseberry Cake with Honey & Thyme Cream
- 243 Leek, Thyme & Butter Bean Gratin
- 159 Lovely Autumn Veg & Grains with a Ginger Soy Dressing
- 246 Miso Onions & Puy Lentils
- 266 Pomegranate & Blood Orange Trifle
- 79   Radish Butter
- 71   Rhubarb & Custard Blondies
- 68   Rhubarb & Pink Peppercorn Crumble
- 202 Ripe Figs, Honey Mascarpone & Pistachio Brittle
- 47   Risi e Bisi
- 170 Roasted Beetroot & Wasabi Soup
- 53   Sausage, Borlotti & Spring Green Casserole
- 62   Spring Onion Scones & Jalapeño Cream Cheese
- 142 Strawberry & Black Pepper Granita, Clotted Cream
- 151 Spicy Sweet Seeds
- 184 Sweet Potato Gratin Pie
- 227 Very Untraditional French Onion Soups
- 48   Wild Garlic Gnudi
- 188 Wild Mushroom Hotpot
- 222 Zesty Kale Salad

DISHES TO GIFT

- 198 Beetroot Velvet Cake
- 263 Blood Orange & Poppy Seed Loaf
- 251 Caramelized Onion & Potato Galette
- 244 Creamy Leek Tart
- 140 Gooseberry Cake with Honey & Thyme Cream
- 68   Rhubarb & Custard Blondies
- 64   Soda Bread
- 62   Spring Onion & Jalapeño Cream Cheese Scones
- 151 Spicy Sweet Seeds
- 184 Sweet Potato Gratin Pie

INDEX

aioli
  chilli 91, **93**
  roasted garlic **102**, 103
almond 25, 98, 103, 140–1
amba 136, **138–9**
apple & ginger tarte tatin **206**, 207
aquafaba 14, 72, 91
artichoke *see* globe artichoke;
  Jerusalem artichoke
asparagus 33, 37
  asparagus tart 22, **23**
  beans al limone with asparagus
    & peas 36
  farinata with asparagus & peas
    30, **31**
  griddled asparagus & caper salsa
    toast 35
aubergine
  aubergine & golden sauce 112–13
  aubergine schnitzel, cucumber
    salad 105–6, **107**
  aubergine stew, whipped tahini
    sauce 118, **119**
  burnt aubergine & chimichurri
    pasta 116
  roasted aubergine 137, **138**
  zhoug & smoky aubergine
    sandwiches 121
autumn recipes 146–208
avocado, charred corn, avocado &
  jalapeño dip 84, **85**

barley & butternut squash bowls,
  halloumi croutons 160, **161**
basil 30, 80, 89, 94, 95, 98, 109, 117,
  123, 127, 182, 241
bean(s) 14, 130–2, 170, 195–6
  bean confit 123
  blistered broad beans, with chilli,
    lime & salt 81
  crispy rice, smashed cucumbers &
    black bean salad 104
  miso red cabbage, mash & crispy
    beans 180, **181**
  runner bean fattoush 100, **101**
  sausage, borlotti & spring green
    casserole **52**, 53
  see butter bean; cannellini bean

beetroot 159
  beetroot velvet cake 198–9, **200–1**
  crimson beetroot dahl 172, **173**
  golden beetroot & fig salad 154, **155**
  roasted beetroot & wasabi soup 170
bellinis, frozen peach 144, **145**
blackberry
  blackberry grilled cheese 152
  blackberry old fashioned 208, **209**
blondies, rhubarb & custard **70**, 71
blood orange
  blood orange & poppy seed
    loaf 263
  blood orange & radicchio salad
    230, 231
  pomegranate & blood orange trifle
    266, **267**
bread, soda bread & wild garlic butter
  64–5, **65**
brie
  blackberry grilled cheese 152
  cheese fondue, Jersey Royals,
    a pickle of pickles **26**, 27
broccoli *see* purple sprouting
  broccoli
bruschetta with maple pears & thyme
  ricotta 215, **217**
Brussels sprout 232–4
  Brussels sprout kinda Caesar
    salad 233
  Brussels sprout pakoras 234, **235**
  gnocchi & sprout gratin 233
  Gruyère & cream sprouts 234, **235**
  honey teriyaki, black sesame &
    sprout udon 260, **261**
  quick, creamy sprout pasta 233
  raw Brussels salad 232
  roasted sprouts 232
  shredded sprout & golden lemon
    salad **235**, 236–7
  sprout, sticky onion & chestnut
    toast 214
  sprout & potato cakes 232
  sprouts & chestnuts 234, **235**
  stir-fried sprouts 233
burrata 30, 94, 98, 214
  persimmon, burrata & chilli crisp
    223, **225**

butter
  brown butter 133
  lemony, buttery sauce 89
  miso butter 192
  radish butter 79
  wild garlic butter 64–5, **65**
butter bean 103, 109, 153, 227
  beans al limone with asparagus
    & peas 36
  leek, thyme & butter bean gratin
    242, 243
  spanakopita beans 120
butternut squash 159, 162
  butternut squash & barley bowls,
    halloumi croutons 160, **161**
  butternut squash & black rice soup
    bowls 168–9

cabbage 157
  colcannon patties 178–9
  griddled hispi cabbage & charred
    jalapeño sauce 171
  miso red cabbage, mash & crispy
    beans 180, **181**
cakes
  beetroot velvet cake 198–9, **200–1**
  blood orange & poppy seed
    loaf 263
  gooseberry cake with honey &
    thyme cream 140–1
cannellini bean 33, 84, 170
  bean confit 123
  burnt leeks & cannellini beans 240
  creamed corn cannellini beans 122
  crispy beans 180, **181**
  purple sprouting broccoli & tahini
    beans 51
caper(s) 103, 109, 137, 259
  caper salsa 35
caramel, miso 268, **269**
carrot & poppy seed salad 90, **92**
casserole, sausage, borlotti & spring
  green **52**, 53
cauliflower 262
  cauliflower gnocchi cheese & a
    green crumb **258**, 259
  griddled za'atar cauliflower & tofu
    cream 241

cavolo nero 167
    cavolo nero curry 174–5
    cavolo nero orzo 193
celeriac 256–7
    celeriac & spelt soup 228, **229**
Cheddar 62, 184–5, 194, 244–5, 246, 251–2
    blackberry grilled cheese 152
    cauliflower gnocchi cheese & a green crumb **258**, 259
cheese 48–50, 61, 128–9, 182, 184–5
    cheese fondue, Jersey Royals, a pickle of pickles **26**, 27
    see also specific cheeses
chestnut 256–7
    sprout, sticky onion & chestnut toast 214
    sprouts & chestnuts 234, **235**
chickpea 90, 118, 130–2, 157, 236–8
    autumn pasta with chickpeas **166**, 167
    herby hummus 262
    hummus 134
    see also aquafaba
chicory, pears & candied thyme walnuts 219, **220–1**
chilli
    blistered broad beans, with chilli 81
    charred peas, mint, chilli, ricotta 32
    chilli aioli 91, **93**
    chilli pangrattato 54, **55**
    persimmon, burrata & chilli crisp 223, **225**
    squash & sweet chilli salad 156
chimichurri & burnt aubergine pasta 116
chive(s) 30
    lemon & chive crème fraiche 228, **229**
chutney, green 56, 57, **58–9**
cocktails
    blackberry old fashioned 208, **209**
    frozen peach bellinis 144, **145**
    the greyhound 270, **271**
    rhubarb sour 72, **73**
coconut 14–15
coconut cream 14–15, 112–13
coconut milk 14–15, 114, 168–9
    lemongrass, coconut, noodles, greens 37, **38–9**
colcannon patties, curry mayo 177, 178–9

compote, rhubarb **70**, 71
confit, bean 123
coriander 57, 84, 104, 121, 130–2, 157, 159, 171
cream 184–5, 188–9, 203, 269
    Gruyère & cream sprouts 234, **235**
    honey & thyme cream 140–1
    pomegranate & blood orange trifle 266, **267**
    strawberry & black pepper granita, clotted cream 142, **143**
cream cheese 22, 127
    cheese fondue **26**, 27
    cream cheese icing 198–9, **200–1**
    jalapeño cream cheese 62, **63**
creamed coconut 14–15, 172
crème fraiche 36, 61
    ginger 206, **207**
    lemon & chive 228, **229**
croutons, halloumi 160, **161**
crumble
    crumble topping 140–1
    rhubarb & pink peppercorn 68, **69**
cucumber 100, 137
    cucumber salad 105–6, **107**
    smashed cucumbers 104
curry
    cavolo nero 174–5, **176**
    curried parsnips, mango halloumi 238, **239**
    curry mayo 177, **178–9**
    curry pastes 37, 112–13
    pumpkin curry 195–6, **197**
    tomato curry, crispy tofu, rice 114, **115**

dahl, beetroot 172, **173**
dill 120, 130–2, 262
dips
    avocado & jalapeño 84, **85**
    for globe artichoke 89
    peanut 218
dressings 90, 98, 100, 154, 157, 219, 231, 236–7
    ginger soy **158**, 159

egg 15, 46, 67, 71, 178–9, 184–5, 269
    jammy eggs 137, **139**
Emmental, cheese fondue **26**, 27

farinata with asparagus & peas 30, **31**
fattoush, runner bean 100, **101**

fennel
    fennel, tomato & salsa verde traybake 108, **109**, **110–11**
    fennel & sausage pappardelle 128–9
feta 100, 120
fig
    fig, honey mascarpone & pistachio brittle 202
    golden beetroot & fig salad 154, **155**
    rice pudding & jammy figs 203, **204–5**
fondue, cheese **26**, 27
foraging 42
fritters, pear fritters & miso caramel **268**, 269

galette, caramelized onion & potato 251–2, **253**
garlic
    new potato & garlic soup 24
    roasted garlic aioli **102**, 103
Georgie Eats 8
ginger
    apple & ginger tarte tatin **206**, 207
    ginger crème fraiche 206, **207**
    ginger soy dressing **158**, 159
globe artichoke 86, **87–8**, 89
gnocchi
    cauliflower gnocchi cheese & a green crumb **258**, 259
    gnocchi & sprout gratin 233
    tomato & gnocchi bake 117
gnudi, wild garlic 48–50, **49**
goat's cheese 154, 156
gooseberry cake with honey & thyme cream 140–1
grains, lovely autumn veg & grains with a ginger soy dressing 159
granita, strawberry & black pepper 142, **143**
gratin
    gnocchi & sprout 233
    leek, thyme & butter bean **242**, 243
greyhound, the 270, **271**
Gruyère 184–5
    Gruyère & cream sprouts 234, **235**

halloumi
    halloumi croutons 160, **161**
    mango halloumi 238, **239**
hazelnut 243, 259
    hazelnut salsa 153

INDEX   283

honey
    honey & thyme cream 140-1
    honey mascarpone 202
    honey teriyaki 260, **261**
    honey-poached rhubarb **66**, 67
hummus 134, **135**, **138-9**
    winter hummus bowl 262

icing, cream cheese 198-9, **200-1**

jacket potatoes, miso butter 192
jalapeño
    avocado & jalapeño dip 84, **85**
    charred jalapeño sauce 171
    jalapeño cream cheese 62, **63**
Jerusalem artichoke 249-50
    crispy pan-fried 226
    roasted Jerusalem artichoke risotto 254

kale 227, 228, 249-50
    zesty kale salad 222
kalettes, five spices kalettes & peanut dip 218
kidney bean 130-2, 195-6

lasagne **248**, 249-50
leek 243
    burnt leeks & cannellini beans 240
    creamy leek tart 244-5
    leek, thyme & butterbean gratin 243
lemon
    beans al limone with asparagus 36
    lemon & chive crème fraiche 228, **229**
    lemony, buttery sauce 89
    shredded sprout & golden lemon salad 235, **236-7**
lemongrass, coconut, noodles, greens 37, **38-9**
lentil(s) 130-2, 188-9, 262
    beetroot dahl 172, **173**
    miso onions & Puy lentils 246, **247**
    rice, lentils, crispy onions 255
lettuce, charred 124, **125**
lime 84
    blistered broad beans, with chilli, lime & salt 81
    lime pickle mayo 28, **29**

mango 136
    curried parsnips, mango halloumi 238, **239**

mascarpone 128-9, 182
    honey 202
mash 180, **181**
mayo
    curry **177**, 178-9
    lime pickle 28, **29**
    roasted garlic aioli 103
menus, seasonal 272-3
milk 15
mint 33, 47, 57, 100, 109, 137, 153, 156, 159, 231, 241
    charred peas, mint, chilli, ricotta 32
miso 104, 168-9, 188-9, 243, 256-7
    miso butter jacket potatoes 192
    miso caramel **268**, 269
    miso onions & Puy lentils 246, **247**
    miso red cabbage 180, **181**
    radishes braised with miso 82, **83**
mozzarella 153, 182, 231, 249-50
mushroom 160
    wild mushroom hotpot 188-9, **190-1**
    wild mushrooms & pickled walnuts with cheesy polenta 194

noodles
    cold peanut noodles & charred lettuce 124, **125**
    honey teriyaki, black sesame & sprout udon 260, **261**
    lemongrass, coconut, noodles, greens 37, **38-9**
    a very herby noodle soup 130-2, **131**

oils 15
old fashioned, blackberry 208, **209**
onion
    caramelized onion & potato galette 251-2, **253**
    crispy onions 255
    miso onions & Puy lentils 246, **247**
    pink pickled onions 195-6, **197**
    very untraditional French onion soup 227
orange 67, 68
    see also blood orange

pakoras, sprout 234, **235**
paneer 174-5
    parathas, paneer, pickled rhubarb, green chutney 56, 57, **58-9**
pangrattato, chilli 54, **55**
panko breadcrumbs 105-6, 236-7

panzanella, peach panzanella salad 98, **99**
parathas, paneer, pickled rhubarb, green chutney 56, 57, **58-9**
Parmesan 36, 41, 43, 48-50, 54, 62, 89, 117, 128-9, 133, 167, 182, 184-5, 194, 240, 249-50, 251-2, 254
parsley 22, 25, 27, 33, 53, 90, 100, 109, 116, 120, 130-2, 137, 188-9, 259, 262
parsnip, curried parsnips, mango halloumi 238, **239**
pasta
    autumn pasta with chickpeas **166**, 167
    baked chard conchiglioni 182, **183**
    burnt aubergine & chimichurri pasta 116
    cavolo nero orzo 193
    fennel & sausage pappardelle 128-9
    herby noodle soup 130-2
    lasagne **248**, 249-50
    purple sprouting broccoli orecchiette & chilli pangrattato 54, **55**
    quick, creamy sprout pasta 233
    samphire & brown butter bucatini 133
    silk handkerchief pasta with wild garlic pesto **44-5**, 46
    slow-cooked courgette tagliatelle **126**, 127
    soupy pasta goodness 34, **35**
    springestrone 33
    wintery pasta 256-7
pastry dishes
    asparagus tart 22, **23**
    caramelized onion & potato galette 251-2, **253**
    creamy leek tart 244-5
    ginger, apple & ginger tarte tatin **206**, 207
    sweet potato gratin pie 184-5, **186-7**
patties, colcannon **177**, 178-9
peach
    frozen peach bellinis 144, **145**
    peach panzanella salad 98, **99**
peanut 159
    cold peanut noodles & charred lettuce 124, **125**
    peanut dip 218
    sticky peanut swede 150

pear
  bruschetta with maple pears
    & thyme ricotta 215, **217**
  chicory, pears & candied thyme
    walnuts 219, **220–1**
  pear fritters & miso caramel
    268, **269**
pea(s) 33
  beans al limone with asparagus &
    peas 36
  charred peas, mint, chilli, ricotta 32
  my farinata with asparagus & peas
    30, **31**
  risi e bisi 47
  spring pea risotto **40**, 41
pepper, potato & roasted garlic aioli
  102, 103
persimmon, burrata & chilli crisp
  223, **225**
pesto
  pesto-esque sauce 89
  wild garlic 43, **44–5**, 46
pickles
  lime pickle mayo 28, **29**
  a pickle of pickles **26**, 27
  pickled radish 136, **139**
  pickled rhubarb 56, 57, **58–9**
  pickled walnuts 194
  pink pickled onions 195–6, **197**
pie, sweet potato gratin 184–5, **186–7**
pine nut 43, 89, 156, 236–7
pistachio 231
  ripe figs, honey mascarpone &
    pistachio brittle 202
pizza, springtime 43
polenta, cheesy 194
pomegranate & blood orange trifle
  266, **267**
poppy seed
  blood orange & poppy seed loaf
    263
  carrot & poppy seed salad 90, **92**
potato 15–16, 109, 188–9
  caramelized onion & potato galette
    251–2, **253**
  cheese fondue, Jersey Royals, a
    pickle of pickles **26**, 27
  colcannon patties, curry mayo
    178–9
  mash 180, **181**
  miso butter jacket potatoes 192
  new potato & garlic soup 24

potatoes, peppers & roasted garlic
  aioli **102**, 103
sprout & potato cakes 232
tartiflette for spring 61
pumpkin 162
  pumpkin curry 195–6, **197**
purée, cavolo nero 174–5, **176**
purple sprouting broccoli 37
  purple sprouting broccoli
    orecchiette & chilli pangrattato
    54, **55**
  purple sprouting broccoli & tahini
    beans 51
  purple sprouting broccoli tempura
    & lime pickle mayo 28, **29**
radicchio & blood orange salad
  230, 231
radish 100
  pickled radish 136, **139**
  radish butter 79
  radishes braised with miso 82, **83**
Reblochon, tartiflette for spring 61
rhubarb
  honey-poached rhubarb **66**, 67
  pickled rhubarb 56, 57, **58–9**
  rhubarb & custard blondies 70, **71**
  rhubarb & pink peppercorn crumble
    68, **69**
  rhubarb sour 72, **73**
rice
  black rice & sweet potato salad 157
  butternut squash & black rice soup
    bowls 168–9
  crispy rice, smashed cucumbers &
    black bean salad 104
  rice, lentils, crispy onions 255
  rice pudding & jammy figs 203,
    204–5
  risi e bisi 47
  roasted Jerusalem artichoke risotto
    254
  spring pea risotto **40**, 41
  tomato curry, crispy tofu, rice
    114, **115**
ricotta 48–50, 182
  charred peas, mint, chilli, ricotta 32
  ricotta stove cakes **66**, 67
  thyme ricotta 215, **217**
risi e bisi 47
risotto
  roasted Jerusalem artichoke 254
  spring pea **40**, 41

rocket 98, 157
runner bean fattoush 100, **101**

sabich 134–7, **135**, **138–9**
sage 167, 249–50, 256–7
  crispy 228, **229**
salads
  black rice & sweet potato 157
  blood orange & radicchio **230**, 231
  Brussels sprout kinda Caesar 233
  carrot & poppy seed 90, **92**
  chopped 137, **159**
  crispy rice, smashed cucumbers &
    black bean 104
  cucumber 105–6, **107**
  golden beetroot & fig 154, **155**
  my favourite summer 94
  peach panzanella 98, **99**
  potatoes, peppers & roasted garlic
    aioli **102**, 103
  raw Brussels 232
  runner bean fattoush 100, **101**
  shredded sprout & golden lemon
    235, 236–7
  squash & sweet chilli 156
  a very simple tomato 95, **97**
  warm squash 153
  zesty kale 222
salsa
  caper 35
  hazelnut 153
  salsa verde **108**, 109, **110–11**
salt 16
samphire & brown butter bucatini 133
sandwiches
  sabich 134–7, **135**, **138–9**
  wild garlic pesto 43
  zhoug & smoky aubergine 121
sauces
  charred jalapeño 171
  golden 112–13
  lemony, buttery 89
  pesto-esque 89
  sweet chilli 156
  tomato 48–50, **49**, 182, **183**
  whipped tahini 118, **119**, 136, **138–9**
sausage
  fennel & sausage pappardelle 128–9
  sausage, borlotti & spring green
    casserole 52, **53**
schnitzel, aubergine 105–6, **107**
scones, spring onion 62, **63**

INDEX   285

seasonal calendars 20–1, 76–7, 148–9, 212–13
seasonal menus 272–3
seasonality 8–11
seed(s) 192
   spicy sweet seeds 151
   see also specific seeds
sesame seed 51, 104
   honey teriyaki, black sesame & sprout udon 260, **261**
soda bread & wild garlic butter 64, **65**
soft cheese, griddled asparagus & caper salsa toast 35
soup
   butternut squash & black rice soup bowls 168–9
   celeriac & spelt soup (with lots of crispy sage) 228, **229**
   new potato & garlic soup 24
   roasted beetroot & wasabi soup 170
   soupy pasta goodness 34, **35**
   springestrone 33
   a very herby noodle soup 130–2, **131**
   very untraditional French onion soup 227
sourdough crumb 116
soy ginger dressing **158**, 159
spanakopita beans 120
spelt & celeriac soup 228, **229**
spice mix 172
spinach 120, 130–2
spring greens 33, 34
   sausage, borlotti & spring green casserole 52, **53**
spring onion
   crispy 130–2, **131**
   scones 62, **63**
spring recipes 18–72
springestrone 33
squash 159, 167
   squash & sweet chilli salad 156
   summer/winter 162
   varieties 162–5
   warm squash salad & hazelnut salsa 153
   see also butternut squash
steaming 16
stew, aubergine 118, **119**
stock 16
stove cakes, ricotta 66, 67

strawberry
   balsamic strawberries & stracciatella 80
   strawberry & black pepper granita, clotted cream 142, **143**
sugar 16
summer recipes 74–144
swede, sticky peanut 150
sweet chilli sauce 156
sweet potato 159
   black rice & sweet potato salad 157
   sweet potato gratin pie 184–5, **186–7**
sweetcorn
   charred corn, avocado & jalapeño dip 84, **85**
   chilli aioli & Thai basil corn 91, **93**
   creamed corn cannellini beans 122
Swiss chard, baked chard conchiglioni 182, **183**
syrups
   blackberry 208, **209**
   rhubarb 72, **73**

tahini 134, 159, 171, 241, 262
   purple sprouting broccoli & tahini beans 51
   tahini yoghurt 121
   whipped tahini sauce 118, **119**, 136, **138–9**
tarte tatin, ginger, apple & ginger **206**, 207
tartiflette for spring **60**, 61
tarts
   asparagus 22, **23**
   creamy leek 244–5
   tarte tatin, ginger, apple & ginger **206**, 207
   wild garlic pesto 43
tempura 28, **29**
teriyaki, honey 260, **261**
toast, sprout, sticky onion & chestnut 214
tofu
   cavolo nero curry 174–5, **176**
   creamy leek tart 244–5
   lemongrass, coconut, noodles, greens 37
   tofu cream 241
   tomato curry, crispy tofu, rice 114, **115**
tomato 53, 94, 98, 118, 123, 137, 195–6

fennel, tomato & salsa verde traybake **108**, 109, **110–11**
tomato & gnocchi bake 117
tomato curry, crispy tofu, rice 114, **115**
tomato salad 95, **97**
tomato sauce 48–50, **49**, 182, **183**
trifle, pomegranate & blood orange 266, **267**

udon, honey teriyaki, black sesame & sprout 260, **261**

vinaigrette 89

walnut 249–50
   chicory, pears & candied thyme walnuts 219, **220–1**
   pickled walnuts 194
wasabi & roasted beetroot soup 170
white chocolate, rhubarb & custard blondies 71
white wine 41, 61, 128–9, 188–9, 194, 227, 240, 254
wild garlic 42
   wild garlic butter 64–5, **65**
   wild garlic gnudi 48–50, **49**
   wild garlic pesto 43, **44–5**, 46
winter recipes 210–70

yoghurt 84, 118, 136, 238
   tahini yoghurt 121

za'atar griddled cauliflower & tofu cream 241
zhoug & smoky aubergine sandwiches 121

First published 2025 by Bluebird
an imprint of Pan Macmillan
The Smithson, 6 Briset Street, London EC1M 5NR
EU representative: Macmillan Publishers Ireland Ltd, 1st Floor,
The Liffey Trust Centre, 117–126 Sheriff Street Upper,
Dublin 1, D01 YC43

Associated companies throughout the world
www.panmacmillan.com

ISBN 978-1-0350-6048-1

Copyright © Georgie Mullen, 2025
Images copyright © Matt Russell, 2025

The right of Georgie Mullen to be identified as the
author of this work has been asserted by her in accordance
with the Copyright, Designs and Patents Act 1988.

All rights reserved. No part of this publication may be reproduced,
stored in a retrieval system, or transmitted, in any form, or by any means
(electronic, mechanical, photocopying, recording or otherwise) without
the prior written permission of the publisher.

Pan Macmillan does not have any control over, or any responsibility for,
any author or third-party websites referred to in or on this book.

1 3 5 7 9 8 6 4 2

A CIP catalogue record for this book is available from the British Library.
Printed and bound in China

Art Direction & Design: Claire Rochford
Illustration: Natalie Savage
Photography: Matt Russell
Food Styling: Esther Clark
Prop Styling: Rachel Vere

This book is sold subject to the condition that it shall not, by way of trade or otherwise,
be lent, hired out, or otherwise circulated without the publisher's prior consent in any
form of binding or cover other than that in which it is published and without a similar
condition including this condition being imposed on the subsequent purchaser.

Visit www.panmacmillan.com to read more about all our books
and to buy them. You will also find features, author interviews and
news of any author events, and you can sign up for e-newsletters
so that you're always first to hear about our new releases.